THE WORLD GOES RAW COOKBOOK

AN INTERNATIONAL COLLECTION OF RAW VEGETARIAN RECIPES

LISA MANN

SQUAREONE
PUBLISHERS

COVER DESIGNER: Jeannie Tudor
COVER PHOTO: Getty Images, Inc.
DECORATIVE INTERIOR ART: Cathy Morrison
INSTRUCTIONAL INTERIOR ART: Vicki Chelf
EDITOR: Michele D'Altorio
TYPESETTER: Gary A. Rosenberg

Square One Publishers
115 Herricks Road
Garden City Park, NY 11040
(516) 535-2010 • (877) 900-BOOK
www.squareonepublishers.com

Library of Congress Cataloging-in-Publication Data

Mann, Lisa.
  The world goes raw cookbook : an international collection of raw
vegetarian recipes / Lisa Mann.
     p. cm.
  Includes index.
  ISBN 978-0-7570-0320-2
  1. Vegetarian cookery. 2. Raw food diet. I. Title.
  TX741.M34 2010
  641.5'636--dc22

                              2010006059

Printed in Canada

10   9   8   7   6   5   4   3   2   1

THE WORLD GOES RAW

COOKBOOK

AN INTERNATIONAL COLLECTION OF RAW VEGETARIAN RECIPES

CONTENTS

To my husband, Richard,
and my boys, Max and Aiden:
For all of the long hours in the kitchen,
the help cleaning up,
the willingness to taste everything,
and for helping to make it all
a great big loving adventure.

ACKNOWLEDGMENTS

A heartfelt thank-you to Grandmy and Juju for igniting the spark of creativity in the kitchen, where it all began. Who would have thought that brownies and brisket could turn into this? You both continue to be endlessly supportive, whatever my project may be.

Thank you to my raw foodie friends Maureen, Mary, Marianne, and Laura. Our fun tasting parties and your honest opinions kept me going throughout my raw food journey.

I would like to extend my deep appreciation to Rudy, Michele, and Marie from Square One Publishers. Thank you for your encouragement and support.

And finally, thank you to my dear family. Richard, your encouragement and support, both in the kitchen and out, means the world to me. Max and Aiden, thanks for being my biggest fans and for believing that your mom is capable of anything. I love you guys.

PREFACE

My pathway towards raw food has been the culmination of a lifelong love affair with both delicious food and great health. Prior to eating a largely raw food diet, my passion for great food and fitness lead me on many adventures in pursuit of great meals and fun physical challenges to face. Whether it was trekking in Patagonia, bicycling in Scotland, or hiking in Italy, there was always wonderful food to accompany the physical activity. Luckily for me, the two balanced out—somehow, finding longer, more exciting and challenging adventures during my travels allowed me to eat heavier, more processed foods without "paying the price."

Things changed when my twin boys were born and I wasn't able to hike for weeks on end or exercise at my whim and pleasure. It seemed like all of that delicious food I had been eating started to catch up with me. I had always followed a largely vegetarian diet with lots of organic fruits and vegetables. But mixed into that diet was also a fair amount of organic cookies and highly processed snack foods. I began to experience many "minor" health concerns, including recur-

ring sinus infections and colds that seemed to last all winter long. Because these ailments weren't considered serious, I didn't pay much attention to them. Before I knew it, I was on countless courses of antibiotics every year to treat one infection or another. Although I continued to try to eat a largely plant-based diet, which was occasionally raw, it didn't seem to be enough to get my body and immune system back in balance.

I had always suspected that my diet may have been playing a role in my cycle of illnesses, but it wasn't until I enrolled in a French culinary school and stopped strictly monitoring my diet that I realized just how negatively all my delicious indulgences were impacting my health and my body. During culinary school, I experienced a great lack of energy that, when combined with my increased consumption of rich, decadent food and my lack of time to exercise, resulted in an even worse cycle of getting sick, being sick, or recovering from being sick. After several months of this cycle I decided to return to my previous vegetarian diet of whole grains, tofu, and vegetables (and the occasional organic cookie)—but that didn't make me feel great either. I began to feel like I was missing out on a healthier, more energetic life.

Previously, I had learned about the healing benefits of a raw food diet, and I often attempted to eat this way. During the raw food periods of my life, I felt great, but I just wasn't able to sustain those eating habits. Most of the food wasn't appealing to me, and the meals that I did find appealing were too difficult to prepare. As a result, I would easily fall back into old habits and would get sick all over again.

Eventually, I realized that in order to be both healthy and content, I needed to find foods that not only satisfied my tastebuds and fit into my lifestyle, but would also fuel my body and help me lead a healthy life. I wanted to wake up in the morning with great energy, and feel like I had the stamina for yoga, hiking, and playing with my kids. I wanted to experience a clear-headedness without having to consume copious amounts of caffeine throughout the day. Just as importantly, I wanted to feel in control of my eating and hunger. Basically, I wanted to feel great, eat great food, and be free of the food cravings that seemed to have so much power over me—does any of this sound familiar?

I became determined to find—and follow—a diet of raw food that not only made me feel healthy and hearty, but tasted gratifying as well. I joyously applied my French culinary skills to raw foods by experimenting in the kitchen until I was able to create enjoyable, easy-to-prepare raw food. At that point I switched to a 100 percent raw food diet, which lasted for several years. I began to experience the energy and vitality that I had craved. My sinus infections and perpetual colds disappeared. The bottom line was that I felt great—better than I had in years.

After eating 100 percent raw for many years, I now find that I can eat cooked food in moderation and still maintain my current health. Presently, I aim for a diet that is 75 percent raw. However, that's not to say I don't veer off course now and then. During the summer, I would say that I often exceed 75 percent, and during the winter months I sometimes dip below it. Regardless, my goal is always to maintain a diet that is 75 percent raw.

Switching to a largely raw food diet improved my health, increased my energy, and changed my outlook on life. My hope is that by writing this book, I can help others in their journey to achieve greater health while eating fantastic food at the same time.

INTRODUCTION

What if you could eat your favorite ethnic foods in abundance and manage to lose weight without counting calories? Even better, what if you could do this while feeling alert and well-rested, having the energy (and the time!) to play with your kids, do your work, and stick to your exercise routine? You would experience a clear-headedness that could turn the insurmountable into the solvable—it might seem too good to be true.

With *The World Goes Raw* as your guide, you can turn the above scenario into a reality. This book will provide you with everything you need to know to prepare and enjoy fantastic ethnic food, all the while sticking to a healthy, raw food diet. It elevates raw vegetarian cuisine to a new level, making it possible for you to prepare healthy gourmet ethnic raw food simply and elegantly in your own kitchen. You can enjoy an array of delicious meals, including Pizza with Roasted Red Bell Peppers and Sun-Dried Tomatoes, Butternut Squash Soup with Walnut Tapenade, and Chocolate Cherry Biscotti—all while feeling fantastic and losing weight.

A raw food is one that has not been cooked or processed. Therefore, a raw food diet is one made up of raw fruits, vegetables, legumes, nuts, seeds, and grains. Foods can be warmed up before they are eaten, as long as the heating temperature does not destroy the foods' enzymes, which are believed to improve digestion, fight disease, and aid in virtually every biological function in the body. However, there is much debate amongst raw food experts over the exact temperature that enzymes are destroyed. While most scientists agree that enzymes cannot live above 118°F, some studies show that enzymes begin to break down at 105°F. Other studies report that enzymes can remain intact at temperatures as high as 140°F, depending on the exact conditions. Variables that affect the temperature that enzymes remain intact are the particular dehydrator used, the water content of the item being heated, and the amount of time that the heat is applied for. For this reason, I recommended dehydrating all items at 105°F to ensure the preservation of the enzymes. By doing this, the foods prepared are still considered raw and therefore can help us on our path to supreme health.

Research has long shown that eating a largely plant-based diet can prevent serious disease, prolong life, and help people feel and look younger. Now, there is also evidence of dramatically increased benefits arising from eating a *raw* plant-based diet. It used to be that eating a healthy and mostly raw vegetarian diet was easi-

1

er said than done. This has created challenges for many people who wanted to eat a largely raw food diet, but didn't want to spend hours in the kitchen preparing the same mundane meals. People want to be able to enjoy the same exquisite cuisine they loved before "going raw"—and finally, there is a way. *The World Goes Raw* is chock full of inspired raw recipes that are so light and delicious, you'll never miss those heavy ethnic foods that used to make you feel bloated or sick.

The first chapter of the book is an introduction to the general concepts of a raw food diet. You will learn how to stock your kitchen with the proper equipment to help make raw food easy to prepare. Instructions on how to use some of the unfamiliar equipment are also included. Additionally, a detailed list of ingredients commonly used on a raw food diet is provided (along with a sample shopping list), so you know exactly what is going into the foods you prepare. Techniques for sprouting, dehydrating, and growing your own glorious kitchen garden are also listed. Finally, I've included tips for effectively organizing your kitchen, ways to introduce your children to the concepts of raw food preparation—letting them in on the fun—and guidelines for making your raw food meals appear as beautiful and appetizing as they possibly can.

The rest of the chapters in the book contain recipes from around the world, each one focusing on a different country or region: Italy, Mexico, the Middle East, Asia, the Caribbean, and South America. Each chapter contains recipes for soups, starters, salads, main courses, and desserts—with a few salad dressings, marinades, and sauces thrown in. At the beginning of each chapter there are suggested menus for both a simple, quick meal (needing no additional equipment), and a more elegant feast (meals that take extra planning and equipment, such as a dehydrator). Keep in mind there are no hard and fast rules for when you can eat what—

you can enjoy a salad as a main course, or a main course as an appetizer. Desserts are so healthy, that you can even enjoy them for breakfast! Let your taste buds and your mood be your guide.

The final sections of *The World Goes Raw* provide resources for hard-to-find materials and other sources of raw food information. You will find metric conversion tables, along with information on where to order kitchen equipment and uncommon ingredients, websites for organizations that offer raw food classes, and a list of books that I recommend to anyone who wants to learn more about raw food, vegetarianism, or the health of our planet.

The World Goes Raw is all about liberation— no longer feeling sick after eating the foods you love, seeing results on the scale (since many people lose weight effortlessly while eating this way), and finally being able to nourish your body and gain control over your hunger and your cravings. Eating a raw, vegetarian diet will open up a whole new world of enjoying food in its most natural and delicious form. You won't believe how good it tastes and how good it makes you feel. Forget about plain nut loaf and sprouted wheatgrass juice—this is raw food cuisine at its finest, adapting classic, ethnic dishes to meet raw food and health standards. The recipes in this book do not only taste fantastic, they will make you feel fantastic as well!

The World Goes Raw will guide you toward a healthier lifestyle, while showing you how to prepare easy and exciting raw global cuisine. Whether you want to be inspired by making raw food that is out of the ordinary, lose weight easily while following a healthy, ethnic diet, or just prepare some divine and healthy raw meals, *The World Goes Raw* is the book for you. With pure pleasure, I invite you to join me in an exploration of this fresh, light style of global cuisine.

1

BaSIcS

Starting a new diet generally stimulates some emotions: determination to succeed, excitement for the potential results, and maybe even a little bit of anxiety or apprehension that things won't go as planned.

Starting a raw food diet often invokes similar emotions, perhaps to a higher degree because a raw food diet is often perceived as more restrictive. However, getting into raw foods needn't be complicated, confusing, or scary. If you have the tools and know the vocabulary, you'll be able to fall into a routine quickly and easily. Once you learn how to prepare beautiful and natural raw meals, you will learn that a raw food diet is actually less restricting than traditional low-calorie diets. Because your body knows exactly how to process food in its natural state, you can eat this delicious food to your heart's content without worrying about counting calories. And because you will be feeding your body such nutritious and delicious food, you will be amazed at how satiated you feel.

After eating raw for many years and helping others with their own raw food journeys, I have learned that properly stocking one's kitchen with essential equipment and ingredients makes it easy and fun to prepare raw food. In this section, you will be introduced to the exciting equipment and staple ingredients that make going raw easy and fun.

EQUIPMENT

In order to successfully start a raw food diet, it is helpful to have the proper equipment to make preparing raw food easy and fun. I've divided this section into two parts, essential equipment and optional equipment. All of the recipes in this book can be prepared using only items from the essential equipment list, but investing in some of the optional equipment will certainly help you prepare beautiful, enticing meals. For those just starting out on a raw food diet, however, sticking to the essentials is just fine.

For ordering information on any of the equipment in this section—both essential and optional—see the Resources section, beginning on page 145.

ESSENTIAL EQUIPMENT

When it comes to equipment, there are a few tools that are essential to preparing raw food, while other tools are beneficial but not necessary to own. The following tools are all essential when embarking on a raw food diet. You may already own some of them, but if you do not it is a very good idea for you to purchase them.

Blender

A blender is an appliance with whirling blades that chop, blend, and liquefy foods. In the beginning of your raw food journey, a basic five-speed blender will be more than adequate. All the recipes in this book that require a blender can be made using just a basic blender, but over time you might find that a high-speed blender is an indispensable tool as well. High-speed blenders are more expensive, often costing upwards of two hundred dollars, but they have highly powered motors that have the ability to make smooth and creamy textures out of items that are harder to chop, like nuts (for soups and sauces) and ice (for ice creams).

Cutting Board

A cutting board is any hard surface that you can cut food on. Wooden cutting boards are easy to use and made from natural material, but you need to pay special attention when cleaning them, as they can harbor bacteria in the small nicks. I prefer to use bamboo cutting boards, as they are also made from natural materials but are harder than wood. Thus, they have less chance of bacterial contamination.

Food Processor

Food processors are containers that have interchangeable rotating blades. They are used for chopping, slicing, shredding, and blending different foods. A simple food processor is an essential piece of equipment to prepare the majority of raw food recipes you will find this book. Owning one that holds at least five cups of food, has a basic "S" blade (a multipurpose blade in the shape of an "S" used for chopping), and a grating blade (a round metal disc with small holes that produce grated vegetables) will be the easiest to use and offers the most versatility.

Sometimes, people ask me why they should invest in both a blender and a food processor, rather than simply using a blender to chop and combine food. It is a good question. While a blender often can chop and mash food to the same consistency a food processor can, each piece of equipment has a unique function. Many times, food processors are more versatile. It is easier to prepare small quantities of food in a food processor, and food processors are generally better at handling solid foods, while blenders are better suited to liquids. Additionally, food processors are often better for controlling how coarsely something is chopped. Raw foodies will definitely benefit from owning a blender and a food processor, since much of raw food meal preparation involves combining solids—which is much easier to do in a food processor.

Grater

A grater is a metal utensil with sharp perforations used for grating foods. I recommend using graters that are in the shape of a tall box, as they provide stability so that fingers don't get accidentally scraped.

Peeler

A peeler is a handheld utensil that is used to peel away outer layers of fruits and vegetables. The blade that is attached to the handle has a small opening in it. Look for peelers that have a "swivel action" handle, which allows the blade to conform easily to the fruit or vegetable it is peeling. Keep in mind that some peelers have specific titles, such as vegetable peelers, potato peelers, or apple peelers, etc. Regardless of what the peeler is called, it can be used on both fruits and vegetables.

OPTIONAL EQUIPMENT

There are some pieces of equipment that are great to have, but are not absolutely essential to preparing raw food. The following equipment will make your "un-cooking" easier and offer more variety in the kinds of dishes that you will be able to prepare, but are not required to prepare any of the recipes in this book.

Chef's Knife

A basic chef's knife has a sharp, curved metal blade that is attached to a handle. The curve of the blade allows for easy cutting and rocking on a cutting board or hard surface. Chef's knives come in many varieties, sizes, and costs. In the beginning of your raw food journey, *any* sharp knife that you own will do the trick, but in time you may want to invest in a knife that is comfortable to hold and allows for quick cutting of your raw foods. I recommend an eight-inch chef's knife with a high-carbon stainless steel blade.

Dehydrator

A dehydrator is essentially an electronically powered box that uses warm air to reduce the water content in food. They come in many varieties and shapes. Some have rows or shelves, and others have only one level for dehydrating. Dehydrator temperatures can be controlled at very precise and low-temperature settings, which allows you to cook items without destroying their natural enzymes, so the food is technically still raw. This allows you to easily prepare items like cookies, breads, and crackers. The result is enzyme-rich food that still tastes like it has been "cooked." Although a dehydrator is a bit of an initial investment, you may start to miss baked goods and breads after an extended period of time on a raw food diet. I recommend an Excalibur (see Figure 1.1, page 6), which can run upwards of one hundred fifty dollars. It is a bit more of an investment, but it will last for years and is easy to use. Cheaper models are generally harder to use and clean. It is a very valuable tool to have.

If you don't own a dehydrator, you can put your oven on the lowest setting (usually around 125°F) and keep the door ajar when food is inside to simulate a dehydrator. While this does not ensure 100 percent that all of the enzymes will remain intact, leaving the door ajar will bring the temperature down to somewhere around the 118°F mark where scientists agree that most enzymes can survive. While I wouldn't recommend this method long-term because it is not energy efficient and isn't exact in temperature, it is a good way to experiment with dehydrating before investing in a dehydrator. Many modern ovens have dehydrators built in, so be sure to check yours.

Conversely, although the dehydrated recipes in this book are best if made with a dehydrator, many of the treats can be eaten as is (without dehydrating) or frozen and eaten later. Dehydrating creates a firmer texture, but all of the recipes in this book are raw, and therefore do not need to be cooked before they can be eaten.

The inset on the next page will explain how to use a dehydrator.

USING A DEHYDRATOR

Dehydrators are like mini-ovens that have exact temperature settings to ensure your food isn't heated over 118°F.

A dehydrator often comes with mesh trays (sometimes called screens) and Teflex sheets (also called non-stick sheets). Check to see if the model you are considering purchasing comes with these—you may need to buy them separately if it does not. The mesh trays look like mesh screens. They should be used when you are dehydrating something that is not gooey and therefore won't fall through the holes (such as Sprouted Chickpea Falafel, page 88). The Teflex sheets are made of a non-stick surface and are placed on top of the screens. They should be used when you are dehydrating something that starts out as a more runny substance (such as Corn Chips, page 64).

For the recipes in this book, the times listed for dehydrating are somewhat approximate, because times will vary depending on how crunchy you prefer your food. Because these recipes do not require ingredients that need to be cooked in order to eat, the food in the dehydrator is deemed "done" when it has reached a texture that you would enjoy eating.

Special care should be taken when flipping over any of the recipes that require "cooking" on both sides, which is the case with most recipes that require a Teflex sheet (for example, pizza crust, page 52). You can tell when something is ready to be flipped over when it comes up easily and does not stick to the Teflex sheet.

Figure 1.1. Excalibur Dehydrator

How to Flip an Item

1. Remove the mesh tray with the Teflex sheet and the item on it from the dehydrator. Cover the item with a second Teflex sheet and then another mesh tray so that you have made a sandwich with the food in the middle.

2. Flip the item over while gently holding the trays together.

3. Gently remove the top tray and Teflex sheet (originally on the bottom) and place the item back in the dehydrator. If, after flipping the trays, the top Teflex sheet (originally the bottom) does not peel off easily, flip the trays back over and place the food in the dehydrator as it was for an additional hour, then try flipping again.

Juicer

Juicers are devices that are used to extract juices from fruits and vegetables. Many people who eat a largely raw food diet use their juicers to make vegetable juice every day. Drinking vegetable juice is an amazing way to pump your body full of vital nutrients and enzymes that it needs without having to consume insurmountable amounts of vegetables. If you choose to buy a juicer, it is important to consider cost (different brands and models range from forty to five hundred dollars) and effectiveness. The main differences in the higher priced models are that they are able to extract more juice from each vegetable (thus pro-

ducing less waste), they are able to extract the juice in a way that is more nutritionally sound, and they are easier to use and clean.

It is also important to consider the difference between a manual juicer and an electric juicer. Manual juicers are the "old fashioned" type of juicers that require users to press down on the fruit in order to extract the juice. Although these are handy devices and sufficient for squeezing orange juice, they are labor-intensive, don't extract much juice, and are only used for citrus fruits. For your raw food needs, it really pays to invest in an electric juicer that does the work for you and can be used on all kinds of fruits as well as vegetables.

USING A JUICER

Juicing your own fruits and vegetables is one of the healthiest gifts that you can give to your body, as it helps release foods' natural enzymes and nutrients in a more digestible form. Drinking this fresh juice is far more nutritious than drinking juice that has been bottled and stored. Most fruits and vegetables can be juiced, with the exception of very dense fruits like avocados, bananas, and papayas.

HELPFUL TIPS FOR USING A JUICER

- Try to buy organic fruits and vegetables.

- Wash all fruits and vegetables thoroughly before juicing. If you aren't using organic fruits and vegetables, consider using a vegetable brush to scrub off any pesticide residue.

- After washing, cut the fruits and vegetables into sizes that will easily fit into the mouth of your juicer, being mindful to remove any large pits.

- With the exception of citrus and other very hard peels, fruit and vegetables can be juiced with their skin on.

- Push the vegetables and fruits through the mouth of the juicer with the appropriate tool

(provided with the juicer) to avoid putting your fingers too close to the blades.

- When juicing denser items like dark, leafy greens or beets, try placing them in between higher water content vegetables to help run produce smoothly through the machine. For example, celery is watery and very easy to juice. Kale is not. Juicing a few stalks of celery, then a few leaves of kale, then a few more stalks of celery will help the juicer run smoothly.

- Enjoy your juice as soon as possible after you are finished juicing, as this is when it is highest in nutrients.

If you are interested in buying the best juicer that extracts the most nutrients from your fruits and vegetables, I recommend a Green Star Juicer. That being said, any juice that you can make for yourself is better than none at all, so you can also start out with much less expensive models. These are far less efficient and won't last as long, but you can still benefit in many ways by drinking juice made with less expensive brands of juicers. When I first converted to a raw food diet, I used an inexpensive brand, since I didn't want to spend so much money on something I wasn't sure that I would use. However, I quickly found that my juicer became a useful tool.

Recently, Jack LaLanne, the fitness guru from days gone by, came out with his own brand of juicers. While they don't extract the most nutrients from green leafy vegetables, they are moderately priced (around $100), easy to use, and easy to clean.

Because I want this book to be accessible to everyone, I want to make it clear that the juicer is not a necessary piece of equipment in order to make any of the recipes. But again, it is a really wonderful addition to any raw food kitchen.

The inset on page 7 will explain how to use a juicer.

Mandolin Slicer

A mandolin slicer is a piece of equipment used to cut fruits and/or vegetables into thin, uniform slices. It consists of a very sharp blade affixed to a plastic or metal board. The height of the blade can be adjusted, depending on how thick or thin you want the slices to be. Some mandolin slicers come with retractable legs that lock the base into place, making it safer and more secure.

This tool is relatively inexpensive and comes in handy when making some of the more delicate recipes in this book, such as Daikon Dumplings (page 103), but it is not essential to own one. You can carefully use your hands and a knife to cut the slices—but they likely won't be as uniform or as thin. If and when you get committed to a raw food lifestyle, you will find the mandolin slicer to be an indispensable tool in making your food preparation easier.

The inset on page 9 will explain how to use a mandolin slicer.

Spiralizer

A spiralizer is a device that allows you to create noodle and spaghetti-like shapes out of vegetables and fruits. There are different types (see Figure 1.3 on page 9), but the one I prefer to use consists of a rotating handle and stainless steel blades that sit on top of a clear, plastic base (the spiralizer on the right in Figure 1.3). Pieces of fruit or vegetable are placed next to the blades, and by turning the handle, they are cut into "noodles" and caught in the base.

A spiralizer is relatively inexpensive. It is great for making zucchini pasta, which can make you feel like you are eating lots of carbohydrates, even though it is just vegetables! If you don't have a spiralizer, you can always use a peeler to make long, flat noodles instead.

The inset on page 9 will teach you how to use the type of spiralizer I prefer.

Whisk

Whisks are manual kitchen tools with long metal or plastic loops attached to a handle. They are used to blend liquids in a fast and airy fashion.

USING A MANDOLIN SLICER

Learning how to safely use a mandolin slicer is one of the most satisfying tricks when learning how to prepare raw foods. While a mandolin slicer certainly isn't necessary, it is great for cutting very thin and uniform slices and helps make speedy work and finely prepared dishes.

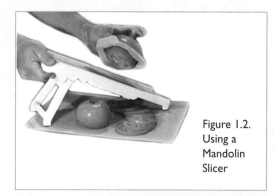

Figure 1.2. Using a Mandolin Slicer

How to Use a Mandolin Slicer

1. Secure the legs of the slicer. Attach a small piece of the food to the protective holder.

2. Adjust the height of the blade on the slicer to determine how thin your slices will be.

3. Brace the slicer with one hand and grab the protective holder (with the vegetable attached to it) in the other hand.

4. With a smooth, forward motion, move the vegetable across the blade of the mandolin slicer (see figure above). Slide the vegetable back, and then bring it forward again, repeating this smooth, steady stroke to make the slices.

USING A SPIRALIZER

It took me several years before I found someone who could show me how to use a spiralizer. Although it may not be obvious at first, once you know how to use one, it is very simple.

Figure 1.3. Two Types of Spiralizers

How to Use a Spiralizer

1. Peel your vegetable and cut it into a 2½-inch long round.

2. Lodge this vegetable wedge into the prongs, located on the bottom face of the top of the spiralizer, attached to the handle.

3. Choose the type of noodles to cut by adjusting the blades in the bottom half.

4. Secure the top half onto the bottom half by fitting the grooves on the sides into one another.

5. As you rotate the handle, it is very important to push firmly on the vegetable. If you don't push down hard while you are turning, the noodles will not form properly. The noodles will pile up in the base of the spiralizer.

INGREDIENTS

When choosing ingredients to make your raw food creations, I recommend buying good-quality organic food, which will simply let the pure flavors shine through. (See the inset on page 14 to learn why buying organic is important.) There are a lot of different ingredients included in this section. Don't panic! It's not necessary for you to purchase them all. For your convenience, a sample shopping list containing the basic ingredients that make up a raw food diet is provided to help you get started (see page 27).

The following is a list of raw food ingredients that are common in many dishes.

VEGETABLES

Eating an abundance of vegetables—particularly green leafy ones such as spinach, kale, and chard—are a staple in any raw food diet and one of the keys to greater health. Vegetables are high in fiber and essential nutrients. Buying locally grown organic vegetables is by far one of the greatest gifts we can give to our bodies, our communities, and the planet. When you buy something, read the label to find out where it was grown. In general, the shorter the amount of time it takes something to travel from the farm to the table, the more nutrients it contains. In addition, there are less stringent laws on pesticide use in other developing countries, so it's worth it to buy food grown in the United States, particularly if the food in question isn't organic. Try to avoid pre-washed vegetables (such as salad greens). These take longer to get to your table, won't last as long in the refrigerator, have more wasteful packaging, and are more expensive. It is worth it to take the extra few minutes to wash unwashed greens.

Try to become familiar with the local farmer's markets in your area. The prices offered are often cheaper than buying from the supermarket, and you can rest assured that the food is locally grown and the money you spend is going directly to the farmers.

The following vegetables are common in most markets and offer a broad range of tastes and nutrients.

ARUGULA. A peppery, somewhat spicy green leafy vegetable.

AVOCADOS. Technically, avocados are a fruit since they form around a large seed, but most refer to them as vegetables. They are shaped roughly like pears and have a green skin that is removed before eating. Avocado varieties and availability vary greatly depending on where you live. Avocados are ripe when they are slightly soft to the touch, but not mushy.

Common avocados are rounder in shape, with medium-green smooth skin. They have a creamy, slightly watery, and mild tasting flesh.

Haas avocados are now becoming widely available. The skin is dark green and bumpy, and they are slightly smaller and more teardrop-shaped than the common variety. Haas avocados have a deep, rich, buttery flavor, and they are creamy and dense in texture.

BEET GREENS. Literally the green leaves that grow from the top of a beet plant, beet greens are best if you buy them while they are still attached to the beet. They taste fantastic when chopped and added to any green salad.

BEETS. These vegetables come in a variety of colors and sizes, and they are high in iron. They are a large, round root with red and green leaves. *Chioggia* is a red and white ringed beet.

Golden beets are beets of a yellowish-orange hue that add fabulous color to any meal.

Red beets are the most common variety of beet found in markets.

BROCCOLI. A dark green, round head of many flowery forms called "florets." Both the florets and the peeled stems are edible.

CABBAGE. A head of rubbery leaves that comes in many varieties, cabbage is high in acidophilus, a necessary and beneficial bacteria for digestion.

Bok choy is common in Chinese cuisine and has thick white stalks and dark green leaves.

Napa cabbage has a tight, elongated head with light green, crinkled leaves.

Red (or purple) cabbage is a tightly packed head with deep reddish-purplish leaves.

Savoy cabbage has a large, loosely packed head of leaves and is light green.

White cabbage is a tightly packed head of leaves that is round and light green.

CARROTS. Carrots are long, pointy roots that are high in carotene, which the body converts to vitamin A. Recently, carrots have become available not only in orange, but pale yellow and red as well.

CAULIFLOWER. Similar in appearance to broccoli, cauliflower has a white, flower-like head and a mild taste.

CELERY. A long, pale-green vegetable that grows in a bunch of multiple stalks, celery is an excellent source of vitamins C and K, which support a healthy immune system.

CHARD. Chard is a dark, leafy green in the beet family. It has large shiny leaves and an earthy taste.

Rainbow chard is chard that is grown in a variety of beautiful colors.

CUCUMBERS. Long, green, and round, cucumbers are vegetables with a tough skin and a slightly sweet juicy interior. For maximum nutritional benefit, choose unwaxed cucumbers and eat them with the skin on.

DAIKON. Traditionally used in Asian cooking, Daikon is in the radish family. It is a long white root that looks similar to a carrot, and has a peppery taste.

DANDELION GREENS. You could conceivably find dandelion greens growing in the wild, but for the purposes of these recipes and your safety, I recommend you buy them in the supermarket. They are dark and narrow leafy greens that are bitter and spicy.

EGGPLANT. Common in Mediterranean and Asian foods, eggplant is a long, deep purple vegetable.

ENDIVE. Endive is a small, light green head of leaves that tastes refreshing and light.

FENNEL. Common in Mediterranean cuisine, fennel is a light green bulb with stalks growing out of its top. It has a light licorice taste.

GARLIC. A small, white head of cloves that grow underground, garlic has a robust and spicy flavor. Some medical studies have reported that garlic can lower cholesterol, reduce blood pressure, and fight bacterial infections.

GINGER. Ginger is a brown-skinned knobby root with white flesh. It has a very sweet and spicy flavor. Some studies report that ginger aids digestion and relieves arthritis pain and inflammation.

JICAMA (pronounced *hik-uh-muh*). Jicama is a large round root with brown skin and a white crunchy center. For consumption, the brown skin is peeled off. The taste is mild, refreshing, and slightly sweet.

KALE. A dark, leafy green vegetable with red or white stems, kale is considered to be one of the most nutrient-dense vegetables. For raw food purposes, I recommend removing the tough woody stem and consuming the green leafy part. Kale is extremely high in vitamin A and calcium, and it is rich in antioxidants, which help the body fight disease and premature aging.

KOHLRABI. A bulbous stem with leaves emerging from it, kohlrabi is in the cabbage family. The peeled stem is the part of that plant that is edible. It has a taste that is similar to broccoli.

LEEKS. With an appearance similar to scallions, leeks are long green and white vegetables. The taste is like a mild, garlic-flavored onion.

LETTUCE. Lettuce comes in many varieties and shapes. Try to avoid iceberg lettuce, as it is very low in nutrients. The more nutritionally sound varieties that are commonly available are as follows.

Green butter lettuce is a large and loose head of lettuce with wide leaves.

Green leaf lettuce is a large, loose head of lettuce that has curly edges and a very mild taste.

Red oak leaf lettuce is a large, loose head of reddish-green leaves with curly edges. The taste is mild and earthy.

MUSHROOMS. Mushrooms are edible fungi that add an earthy, sometimes meaty texture to raw foods. Mushrooms are high in potassium and selenium, a potential cancer-fighting nutrient. To prevent them from getting too tough, all mushrooms should be wiped clean with a damp cloth,

as opposed to washing. They come in many varieties, and for safety purposes, should always be bought in the supermarket.

Crimini mushrooms are baby portabella mushrooms.

Portabella mushrooms are large and meaty. Remove the stems before serving.

Shitake mushrooms have a rich, deep flavor. Remove the stems before consuming.

MUSTARD GREENS. Mustard greens are spicy, long, dark green leaves. They taste peppery and tart, and are high in vitamins A and B.

ONIONS. Round and bulbous with many layers, onions come in many varieties and flavors.

Pearl onions are tiny (about one inch in diameter), sweet, and mild.

Red onions have a spicy flavor and a red skin.

Spanish onions have a yellow skin, are large in size, and are somewhat spicy and strong in flavor. They are slightly sweeter, larger and milder than yellow onions.

Sweet onions are mild and crisp, and are often the onions of choice for raw food preparation. There are several different varieties, often named after the region in which they are grown. The most popular include Carzalia, Sweet Imperial, Texas Spring Sweet, Vidalia, and Walla Walla. Sweet onions are seasonal, and are usually available from March through August.

White onions have a white skin and a very sweet and mild flavor. These are often called for in Hispanic dishes, since they have a cleaner, tangier flavor than yellow onions. White globe onions are a popular white onion variety.

Yellow onions are what most cooks reach for when a recipe simply calls for an "onion." Yellow globe onions and yellow storage onions are two common types of yellow onions. The high sulfur content in yellow onions is what makes you tear up when you cut into it. They are very pungent to eat raw.

PARSNIPS. Parsnips are long, off-white root vegetables. They are somewhat earthy and sweet in taste.

PEAS. Peas are a round, green legume. (Legumes are the classification of plants that have seed pods that split in half. The most common legumes are peas and beans.) They are very sweet and light in flavor.

PEPPERS. Peppers encompass a range of vegetables that come in a wide variety of colors, from red and green, to purple and orange. They consist of a fleshy, juicy covering that surrounds many small seeds and ribs on the interior. In general, peppers can be grouped into two categories: hot and sweet.

Hot peppers are peppers of varying spiciness that are usually long (one to three inches in length) and colored green, red, or orange. The heat of the peppers is concentrated on the white ribs inside and in the seeds. The most common types of hot peppers are Anaheim peppers, which are long, thin, light green, and mildly spicy; habanero peppers, which are small, red or orange, and extremely hot; and jalapeño peppers, which are medium-sized, dark green, and moderately spicy.

Sweet peppers are members of the nightshade family (plants that grow at night). They are somewhat circular shaped, with four or five lobes inside. They have a shiny exterior and a hollow interior with seeds inside. The seeds and

white ribs should be removed before eating. The most common types of sweet peppers are green peppers, which are large, mildly sweet, and crunchy; orange peppers, which are large, orange, and very sweet; purple peppers, which are large, deep purple, and somewhat bland tasting; and yellow peppers, which are large, yellow, sweet, and juicy.

RADICCHIO. Radicchio is a small red head of lettuce-like leaves with a white center. It is mildly tart and refreshing.

SCALLIONS. Scallions are bulb-like plants with long green shoots. They are fresh, peppery, and spicy in flavor.

SHALLOTS. Small bulbs with brown skin and white, layered flesh, shallots taste like a cross between spicy onions and mild garlic.

SPINACH. Spinach is a dark green, leafy vegetable that grows as individual leaves. Its flavors are rich, earthy, and versatile.

SQUASH. Technically, squash are the fruits of various members of the gourd family, although we typically refer to squash as a vegetable. Although there are many more varieties of squash available, I have limited the varieties below to those that are easy to prepare when eating raw.

Acorn squash are easily found in supermarkets. This hard winter squash has a green skin and, as its name suggests, is shaped like an acorn.

Butternut squash are easily found in supermarkets. They are beige colored, shaped like a vase, and have a taste somewhat similar to sweet potatoes.

Yellow squash is a long yellow vegetable with a soft center and seeds inside. The flavor is mildly sweet.

SWEET POTATOES. Edible roots belonging to the morning-glory family, sweet potatoes come in many varieties. The two that are widely grown are a pale sweet potato and a darker-skinned variety. Often, the sweet potato is referred to as a "yam," even though the true yam is not related at all to a sweet potato.

Orange sweet potatoes (often labeled as "yams" in the market) have a thick, dark orange skin and a vivid orange, sweet flesh.

White sweet potatoes have a thin, light yellow skin and a pale-yellow flesh. Their flavor is not extremely sweet and the texture is dry and crumbly, much like a white baking potato.

TOMATILLOS. Tomatillos are small, round, fruit-like, green vegetables that resemble green tomatoes with a husk (a thin paper-like covering).

When purchasing tomatillos, look for a fresh green husk and a firm fruit. The only edible part of the tomatillo is the fruity tomato itself. They are crisp and tart-tasting, and common in Mexican cuisine.

TOMATOES. In actuality, tomatoes are a fruit, but they are more commonly referred to as a vegetable. Tomatoes are a round and sweet and are grown in an array of shapes and colors. The emergence of flavorful and visually-appealing varieties of tomatoes has increased, and the types available usually depend on the region and the time of year. I encourage you to try new varieties. The following are a few of my favorites.

Beefsteak tomatoes are large and red.

Cherry tomatoes are small, round, extremely sweet, and red.

Heirloom tomatoes refer to varieties of tomatoes that have been passed down through several generations of a family who continue to grow a spe-

BUYING ORGANIC

Organic foods are better for you for a variety of reasons. They contain no pesticides, and are more nutrient-packed than their non-organic counterparts. However, buying only organic vegetables and fruits can be expensive.

If buying only organic is not an option financially, that is fine. However, some produce simply contain too many pesticides. These specific vegetables and fruits should be bought organic whenever possible. The list below consists of these fruits and vegetables.

- Apples
- Cantaloupe
- Carrots
- Celery
- Cherries
- Grapes
- Lettuce
- Nectarines
- Peaches
- Pears
- Potatoes
- Raspberries
- Spinach
- Strawberries
- Tomatoes

cific variety because of its valued characteristics. Typically, when a tomato is called an heirloom, it also means that no genetically modified organism has been used in its production. These tomatoes are growing in popularity and availability. They are often available in commercial supermarkets, organic grocery stores, and local farmers markets.

Pear tomatoes are extremely sweet, pear-shaped, and are either red, yellow, or orange.

Plum tomatoes are medium-sized and red with a thick flesh and a small amount of pulp.

TURNIPS. Turnips are large, white, round roots, often with purplish edges. They are somewhat bitter and spicy.

WATERCRESS. Watercress has small, round leaves and is sold in bunches. It is high in vitamin C, iron, and calcium. Recent studies have also shown that daily consumption of watercress is linked with a reduction of DNA damage to blood cells, which can reduce the risk of cancer development.

ZUCCHINI. A long, green vegetable that resembles a cucumber, zucchini has a mild and earthy flavor.

FRESH FRUITS

Fruits are the fleshy, sweet part of a plant that form around the center of a flower. They are Mother Nature's way of protecting and feeding the seeds inside. Fruits come in a variety of tastes, textures, and colors, and are a fantastic way of satisfying your sweet tooth without consuming processed foods. If possible, buy organic fruits whenever they are available. Being labeled as "organic" signifies that the food has gone through a lengthy and sometimes costly certifica-

tion process. However, if buying organic isn't an option, look for fruits that have been grown locally, and possibly labeled as "pesticide free."

Additionally, be sure to properly wash your fruits (and vegetables, for that matter) before you consume them. See the inset on page 16 for washing instructions and tips.

The following fruits are common in most markets and offer a broad range of tastes and nutrients.

APPLES. Apples are round, colored fruits that are grown in a surprisingly large variety of species. They are a perfectly "packaged" raw food, as you can bring them anyplace and always have a raw snack on hand. Try experimenting with different varieties if you are used to eating only one type of apple, as the tastes can vary quite a bit from variety to variety. Below are some of my favorites.

Fuji is a delightfully crisp, juicy, and sweet apple with reddish-green skin.

Gala is a medium-red apple with hints of yellow. It is crisp and juicy.

Golden Delicious is a yellowish-green apple that is mildly sweet.

Granny Smith is a green, very crisp apple with a tart taste.

Pink Lady is a red apple with a bit of green. It is tart, slightly sweet, and crisp with hints of rose petal aroma.

APRICOTS. An apricot is a small, orange fruit with a large pit inside. It is sweet, fleshy, and high in beta-carotene (the plant form of vitamin A, which is an antioxidant).

ASIAN PEARS. Asian pears look like large greenish-brown apples. They are incredibly juicy and crisp with a mild, sweet flavor.

HOW TO SAFELY WASH
YOUR VEGETABLES AND FRUITS

According to the Food and Drug Administration (FDA), roughly 12 percent of all food-borne illnesses that occurred between 1990 and 2000 originated in fresh produce. In some of these outbreaks that were widespread, the contamination was likely to have originated at the farm where the product was grown or in the processing plant. (Remember the 2006 recall of spinach due to E. coli contamination that was traced back to the farms where it was grown?)

However, the benefits of eating fruits and vegetables still outweigh the drawbacks. Still, there are certain precautions that we can take to make our food as safe and pure as possible before we consume it.

1. Wash your hands thoroughly before preparing food. This seems simple enough, but it is amazing how easy it is to forget if you aren't in the habit.

2. Wash all fruits and vegetables in cool running water. Be sure to remove all apparent dirt and residues.

3. Consider making a vegetable wash at home if you want to be extra safe. There are many chlorine rinses and "vegetable safe" washes on the market for cleaning fruits and vegetables. Yet, studies have reported that at best, these chemical washes are only slightly more effective at removing harmful residues than the home-made washes in this section. Thus, it is questionable whether these are really worth the cost and extra chemicals. If you want to be extra safe, wash your vegetables and fruits in the following homemade washes instead of investing money in chemical washes.

- For a general, all-purpose wash, mix one tablespoon lemon juice with two quarts of water. Soak vegetables and fruits in this for five minutes and rinse with cool water.

- To eliminate extra residue, sprinkle two tablespoons of table salt into one quart of water and add one-fourth cup of white vinegar. Soak particularly dirty vegetables in this for thirty minutes and rinse thoroughly with cool water.

4. Remove the outer layer if necessary. If the outside leaves of green leafy vegetables look at all dirty, simply remove the outer layer before washing and consuming.

5. Don't exclude vegetables and fruits that you peel. When you slice vegetables and fruits, bacteria and/or pesticides can be transferred from the peel or rind to your hands or to a knife and then to the fruit or vegetable you are preparing. Washing before you peel reduces that risk.

6. Always rewash bagged products. Even if the packaging says "prewashed," extra handling means extra contamination, so it pays to be extra careful.

7. Clean your countertop, cutting boards, and utensils with hot soapy water. Even if you wash your produce, cutting them with dirty utensils or on dirty surfaces will counteract all your other efforts.

BANANAS. Bananas are long, curved, sweet yellow fruits. They are impressively high in potassium, a necessary nutrient.

BERRIES. Berries are small, sweet fruits that come in a variety of shapes and colors. Berries are most flavorful when purchased during their particular season, which varies depending on the region. Berry season begins in the spring and lasts through the fall.

Blackberries are a very seedy black fruit with a sour taste.

Blueberries are a small, round, deep blue fruit that are very sweet when soft and ripe.

Boysenberries are sweet and purple.

Gooseberries are green and are related to the blueberry.

Raspberries are usually red, but occasionally golden raspberries are available in the fall. They are intensely sweet and juicy.

Strawberries are pointed, large, red berries that are sweet. They are high in vitamin C and iron.

CHERRIES. Cherries can either be sweet or sour. These earthy, small red fruits grow on trees and have a small pit inside. Cherries are grown in several varieties of varying sweetness, depending on the region.

FIGS. Often, figs are available as a dried fruit. Fresh figs are small-to-medium sized teardrop-shaped fruits that are greenish-brown on the outside and packed full of tiny seeds on the inside. They are mild, sweet, and earthy-flavored.

GRAPEFRUITS. Grapefruits are medium-sized citrus fruits with yellow skin that is peeled before consuming. They are rich in vitamin C, which can keep your immune system healthy and prevent colds and flu.

Pink grapefruits have pink flesh and are sweet and sometimes mildly tart.

Red grapefruits have a ruby red-colored flesh with yellow skin. They can be very sweet.

White grapefruits are yellow-skinned fruits with white and slightly tart flesh.

GRAPES. Grapes are small, round fruits that grow on vines. Black and red grapes are high in resveratrol, an antioxidant and cancer-preventing ingredient.

Black grapes, such as Concord grapes, typically appear dark purple to black in color, are very sweet, and may have pits inside.

Red grapes are red in color and sweet, as in Red Globe table grapes.

White grapes are light green in color and are often seedless, sweet, and mild in flavor, as in California seedless or Thompson seedless grapes.

GUAVA. Guava are hard, yellow, tropical fruits that are pink on the inside and full of small seeds.

KIWI. Kiwis are small, brown, hairy fruits with vibrant green insides that are filled with edible black seeds. The taste is almost like a strawberry, melon, and banana combined, and the texture is similar to a plum. They are delightfully refreshing and high in vitamin C, a necessary nutrient to support a healthy immune system. The brown skin is edible and contains fiber, but most people prefer to peel it off before eating.

LEMONS. Lemons are small-to-medium sized yellow citrus fruits, and are quite sour in taste.

LIMES. Limes are a small-to-medium sized green citrus fruit, and are sour in taste with bitter undertones.

MANGOS. Mangos are orange-yellow and green

tropical fruits, and have a large pit in the center. The skin is waxy and should be peeled before consuming. They have a superbly sweet and flowery aroma.

MELONS. Melons are large, round fruits with hard skin and seeds on the inside. They contain high amounts of vitamin C. To check if a melon is ripe, look to see if the blossom end (the small brown circle where the vine was attached) is slightly soft and fragrant.

Cantaloupe has a light brown exterior that is slightly bumpy. The interior is bright orange and somewhat sweet.

Casaba has a wrinkled, pale yellow skin with a white, sweet, fleshy interior.

Christmas is an oblong melon with green and yellow stripes and a mildly sweet taste.

Honeydew is a smooth-skinned, very light green round melon with an intensely sweet, light green flesh.

Muskmelons usually grow on the eastern coast of the United States. They have a dense bumpy "net" of skin on the outside and are musky in flavor.

Watermelons can be round or oblong in shape and have green and yellow striped smooth skin. They are juicy and sweet in flavor.

NECTARINES. Nectarines are smooth-skinned, red or yellow fruits with large pits inside. The flesh is white-to-yellow and they are intensely sweet and fragrant.

ORANGES. As the name implies, oranges are a bright orange citrus fruit, and are high in vitamin C.

Blood oranges have red insides and are sweet with earthy undertones.

Clementines are tangy and juicy.

Mineolas are very juicy, sweet, and easy to peel.

Navel oranges are widely available. They are large, seedless, and sweet.

Tangelos are a cross between an orange and a tangerine.

Tangerines are darker orange in color and very sweet inside. The shape is of a somewhat flattened orange.

PASSION FRUIT. Passion fruit is a small-to-medium sized yellow, wrinkled fruit. The insides contain incredibly flavorful and sweet edible seeds and pulp. You know they are ripe when they are very soft to the touch, but not mushy. To eat them, simply cut the fruit in half and spoon out the edible insides.

PEACHES. Peaches are fuzzy, medium-sized fruits with large pits on the inside. They are intensely sweet, and are soft to the touch when ripe.

PEARS. Pears are sweet, medium-sized fruits that are round on the bottom and pointy on the top. The skin can be green, red, brown, or yellow. Some studies report that pears can lower cholesterol levels and promote cardiovascular health.

Anjou pears have green skin and are best when eaten soft.

Bartlett pears are red-skinned and sweet.

Bosc pears are brown-skinned and can be eaten when slightly hard and crispy.

PERSIMMON. Persimmon look like bright orange apples. They are velvety and sweet tasting. Fuyu is the variety that is commonly available and can be eaten hard or soft.

PINEAPPLE. Pineapples are very juicy fruits with a crown of sharp leaves on top. They are ripe when the top leaves can be pulled out easily and the outer skin is slightly soft to the touch. They are high in vitamin C, and the core contains an important digestive enzyme called bromelian.

PLUMS. Plums are small-to-medium sized fruits that are dark purple or red. They can act as a natural laxative.

DRIED FRUITS

Dried fruits are simply fresh fruits that have been dried over time. Virtually any fruit can be dried. When purchasing dried fruits, it is important to read the label and buy unsulfured varieties, which means that they haven't been treated with any chemicals to preserve the color. When fruits are dried, they naturally become super-sweet as the fruit sugars crystallize. Therefore, it is important to buy unsweetened dried fruits with no additional sugar added. Even then, the fruits are sweet enough to replace less healthy sweeteners in many recipes. Be sure to look for organic dried fruits whenever possible.

Currently, there is limited enforcement regarding the temperatures used to dry fruits. This is why it is so important to check labels. Labels that indicate that fruits have been dried at low heats or in the sun are best. When in doubt, buy organic and consume in limited quantities.

This section includes my favorite dried fruits that are generally readily available.

APPLES. Dried apples are an easy and satisfying snack food. They are a favorite, amongst children especially.

APRICOTS. Unsulfured, dried apricots are dark, orange-brown and supremely sweet.

CHERRIES. Dried cherries are a sweet and fun snack food. They often have sugar added, so be sure to read the label carefully.

COCONUT. Dried coconut is simply mature coconut meat that has been dried and shredded. Coconuts are high in healthy saturated fat, with a fair amount of protein and low amounts of sugars.

CRANBERRIES. Dried cranberries are great additions for salads.

DATES. Dates are small, long, brown fruits from date trees. They can be used as a sweetening agent in many raw food dessert recipes.

Deglet Noor are amber colored, sweet, and dry in texture.

Medjool dates are softer and juicier in texture, dark brown in color, and supremely sweet.

FIGS. Dried figs are teardrop-shaped brown fruits. They are very sweet and high in calcium, which protects bone density.

GOJI BERRIES. Dried goji berries have a mild and tangy taste, which is slightly sweet and slightly sour. They are deep red, small berries that come from a shrub and are grown in the Himalayas, Tibet, and China. They are rich in antioxidants, which could prevent the development of cancer cells and promote longevity.

MANGO. Dried mango is made from drying whole mangos and slicing them thin. They are very sweet, making them a favorite amongst young children.

PRUNES. Dried prunes are derived from dried

whole plums. They can work as a great laxative and as a sweetener.

RAISINS. Raisins are made from drying whole grapes. They are an easy and versatile snack for all ages. Raisin varieties depend on the type of grape used. Avoid golden raisins, as they have been treated with sulfur dioxide to obtain the color.

SUN-DRIED TOMATOES. Sun-dried tomatoes are made from whole tomatoes that have been dried over time in the sun. They appear flattened, red, and circular-shaped, are very sweet, and can add a deep and earthy flavor to many raw food dishes. When shopping, be sure to look for pure sun-dried tomatoes as opposed to those packed in oil or preservatives.

FRESH HERBS AND SPICES

Herbs are the flowers and greens of plants that bloom each year. They are a fantastic way to add fresh flavor to any raw food dish. When possible, buy organic herbs or grow your own (see Growing Your Own Kitchen Garden on page 29). Spices are used to give flavor and seasoning to meals.

The following is a comprehensive list of a variety of fresh herbs that are readily available in most supermarkets.

BASIL. Basil is a very aromatic and often sweet herb that grows easily in sunny spots. Try experimenting with different varieties, such as Purple basil, Thai basil, and Lemon basil. It is a common ingredient in both Italian and Thai food.

CHIVES. Chives are the smallest species of the onion family, and they have a mild onion flavor. They are long green stalks that resemble hollow blades of grass.

CILANTRO. A flat-leafed plant with jagged edges, cilantro looks very similar to parsley and is sometimes called Mexican parsley or Chinese parsley. Its flavor is peppery and fresh.

DILL. Dill is a wispy, light green herb. It has a refreshing, mild flavor.

GARLIC. Technically, garlic is a bulb. It has a white, papery skin that is removed before eating, and many cloves forming a pointed, circular shape. The taste is strong and spicy.

GINGER. Although it is technically a root, ginger is commonly referred to as a spice. It looks like a light brown, gnarled root. The skin is peeled before eating. Ginger's spicy, tangy interior is a common flavor in Asian cooking.

MINT. Mint is a refreshing, pointed-oval shaped green leaf that adds great flavor to dishes and is easy to grow.

OREGANO. Oregano is a small, leafed, sharp-flavored herb that is common in Italian cooking.

PARSLEY. Parsley is a jagged, leafed herb that is available in either a flat (also called Italian) or curly leaf variety. Its taste is light and clean.

ROSEMARY. Rosemary has needle-like leaves that grow on woody stalks. Rosemary is easy to grow, and can withstand many different gardening conditions. Its flavor is piney and minty.

SAGE. Sage has long, white, fuzzy round leaves. Its flavor is very aromatic, strong, and earthy.

THYME. Common in French and Italian cooking, thyme has an earthy, subtle flavor. Its leaves are tiny and round and grow on woody stalks.

DRIED HERBS AND SPICES

Like fresh herbs, dried herbs and spices can and add enormous flavor to meals. Most have a shelf life of about six months, after which they begin to lose their flavor. Herbs and spices that are not labeled as organic have most likely been irradiated or exposed to levels of ionizing radiation (as in x-rays) to preserve shelf life and destroy bacteria. Some alternative health practitioners believe that this process is harmful, and that the nutritional benefits of the spices are lost as a result. So, if possible, look to buy organic spices. If they are prohibitively expensive, or if you won't be using a certain herb or spice all that often, look for it in the bulk food section of your local health food store. This will allow you to buy smaller quantities so that they won't go stale while you are storing them.

If you are having trouble finding any of the herbs and spices used in this book, check the Resources section (beginning on page 145) to find out where you can order them.

ALLSPICE. Allspice is made from the dark brown berries on evergreen pimento trees. The flavor resembles a mixture of cinnamon, cloves, and nutmeg.

ANISE SEED. Anise seeds look like tiny, brownish-green commas. They are the seeds from anise plants, and the flavor is sweet and licorice-like.

BASIL. Basil is from the crushed, dried leaves of a basil plant. The flavor is sweet, aromatic, and peppery.

CARAWAY SEEDS. A member of the parsley family, caraway seeds are dry and dark brown. The flavor is nutty, and often associated with the seeds on rye bread.

CARDAMOM SPICE. Cardamom spice is from the ginger family. Its flavor is sweet and pungent. It is a common ingredient in Turkish coffee and coffee cakes.

CAYENNE. Cayenne can be derived from any number of hot red bell peppers. These crushed red bell pepper flakes are very hot and spicy.

CHILI POWDER. Chili powder is the grown, dried spice made from chilies, coriander, cumin, and oregano. This spice can be mild to hot, depending on the variety.

CHIPOTLE PEPPER. Derived from a smoked and crushed jalapeño chili pepper, chipotle pepper intensely smoky, earthy, spicy, and slightly sweet. It is common in Mexican cuisine.

CINNAMON. Cinnamon is derived from bark from a Ceylon or Cassia tree. The flavor is aromatic and sweet.

CLOVES. Cloves are reddish-brown, nail-shaped buds from clove trees, which grow in the tropics. Their flavor is aromatic and sweet and is often associated with holiday baking.

CORIANDER. Coriander is the dried seed from the cilantro herb. Its flavor is bright and distinctive.

CUMIN. Cumin has a flavor that is smoky and warm. It is derived from a bud of a plant in the parsley family, and is common in Middle Eastern foods.

CURRY POWDER. Curry powder is a mixture of spices common in Indian and Asian cuisine. The variety of spices can vary widely depending on where the particular dish has originated, but in the United States curry powder is most commonly a mixture of coriander, cumin, turmeric, and fenugreek. However, many additional spices could be added, such as ginger, garlic, cinnamon, and cloves.

DILL. Dill is simply the dried dill herb, and has a flavor often associated with dill pickles.

FENNEL. Greenish-brown in color, dried fennel is the seed from a fennel plant. The flavor, common in Indian cooking, is aromatic and slightly similar to licorice.

FENUGREEK. Fenugreek seeds are common in many curry recipes. The flavor is slightly bitter and slightly sweet.

MINT. The dried mint herb is made from the dried leaves of a mint plant. There are over twenty-five varieties of mint plants, but the most common are spearmint and peppermint. The flavor of mint is cool and sweet.

MUSTARD SEEDS. Mustard seeds are tiny round seeds that are either white or brown. The brown is stronger in flavor, which is earthy and spicy.

NUTMEG. Nutmeg comes from the ground seed of a nutmeg tree. It has a warm and sweet flavor.

OREGANO. Oregano comes from the dried leaves of the oregano plant. Its flavor is pungent and reminiscent of pizza. It is related to marjoram and thyme.

PAPRIKA. Paprika comes from dried, sweet red bell peppers that are ground into a powder.

Hungarian paprika has a slightly sweet, pungent flavor. This is the variety most commonly found in stores.

Smoked Spanish paprika is made from smoked sweet red bell peppers. It adds a very smoky, earthy flavor to any dish.

PARSLEY. Made from the dried leaves and stems of a parsley plant, parsley's flavor is delicate and fresh.

PEPPERCORNS. Peppercorns (commonly referred to as "pepper") are the most widely used spice. Pepper is derived from the berries from a pepper plant. They can either be purchased whole, crushed, or ground and are available in black, red, green, or white. Peppercorns have a spicy flavor.

ROSEMARY. Rosemary is derived from drying the silver and green needles of a rosemary plant. The flavor is piney and somewhat minty.

SAGE. Sage is derived from the dried, fuzzy, light green leaves of a sage plant. The flavor is musty and slightly bitter.

SEA SALT. Sea salt is salt that is unrefined and harvested directly from the sea. It contains over seventy traces of vitamins and minerals that are vital to good health. (Iodized refined table salt comes from mines, and is heated at high temperatures, which alters its chemical composition.) I prefer using sea salt as opposed to iodized salt, as it is salt in its most natural, unrefined form.

TARRAGON. Tarragon is derived from drying the pointed, dark green leaves of a tarragon plant. The flavor is mild with a hint of licorice, and is common in French cooking.

THYME. Thyme comes from the dried leaves of a thyme bush. The flavor, common in Italian cooking, is slightly minty and tea-like.

TURMERIC. A slightly bitter and earthy spice, turmeric is derived form the root of a plant in the ginger family. It is often used in Indian food to not only enhance the flavor of food, but also the color, which is a deep, golden yellow.

SEA VEGETABLES

Sea vegetables are plants that have been harvested from the sea. They contain, ounce per ounce, an enormous range of minerals, which are virtually all of the minerals that are found in the ocean. Sea vegetables come in many varieties, and below are some of the most common raw food staples. When shopping, be sure to look for "raw" and "untoasted" on the labels (information on where to order these vegetables can be found in the Resources section, beginning on page 145).

DULSE. Dulse is a leafy purple plant that is harvested from North Atlantic seas. It can be eaten dried or rehydrated (by soaking in water until softened). It has a very high iron concentration and is great when sprinkled on salads to add extra flavor and nutrients.

HIZIKI. Hijiki is a black, stringy seaweed. It has a strong flavor and is very high in calcium.

KELP NOODLES. Kelp noodles are clear noodles made from 100 percent kelp. They are chewy, neutral tasting, and a great substitute for pastas.

KOMBU. Kombu is the tradional Japanese name for the seaweed that comes from edible kelp. It is green, sweet, chewy, and very high in potassium.

NORI. Nori is a sea vegetable that is shredded and dried into sheets most commonly used to make sushi. It is rich in calcium, which supports bone density.

WAKAME. Wakame is sweet-tasting seaweed that is light green in color when rehydrated.

NUTS AND SEEDS

Raw nuts and seeds are an important source of protein when following a largely raw food and plant-based diet. Nuts are the edible center of a fruit, and are surrounded by an inedible, hard shell. Seeds are contained inside of the fruits, and are literally the potential energy for a new plant. Thus, seeds contain concentrated amounts of nutrients.

When shopping, always buy raw, untoasted nuts and seeds. This ensures that they are more easily digestible and free from hydrogenated oils and extra fats. When your wallet allows, buy organic. Nuts vary greatly in price; so if you are on a budget, consider keeping less expensive nuts and seeds on hand, such as sunflower and pumpkin seeds. Depending on how much oil is naturally found in the nut or seed, some can go rancid in a few months if not consumed. For maximum nutritional value and freshness, store nuts and seeds in an airtight container in the refrigerator.

ALMONDS. Almonds are brown, oblong in shape, and pointed at one end. They contain high amounts of vitamin E, which is an antioxidant that has been reported to fight cancer and heart disease.

BRAZIL NUTS. Brazil nuts are large, brown, and creamy. They contain high amounts of the mineral phosphorous, which has been reported to boost energy and metabolism.

CASHEWS. Cashews are white, crescent-shaped nuts that are sweet and filling.

FLAX SEEDS. Flax seeds provide a balance of omega oils and essential fatty acids, and are a good source of fiber. They are small and brown.

HAZELNUTS. Often called "filberts," hazelnuts are round and look like brown- skinned chickpeas.

HEMP SEEDS. Hemp seeds are high-protein seeds that contain all nine of the essential amino acids. They are small, flat, and white, and taste great sprinkled on top of salads.

MACADAMIA NUTS. Macadamia nuts are very rich, sweet nuts that are white and round. There is a hint of coconut in the flavor.

PEANUTS. Technically, peanuts are a legume and are therefore in the bean family, but they are most commonly referred to as a nut. Although high in protein, peanuts are controversial. Not only were they associated with salmonella outbreaks, but also because when peanuts grow they can harbor a cancer-causing mold. For this reason, most raw food advocates limit or restrict their consumption of peanuts.

PECANS. Pecans are sweet, oblong-shaped brown nuts. The insides are wavy and resemble walnuts. Pecans are high in vitamin B1 and zinc.

PINE NUTS. Pine nuts are the seeds that come from the insides of cones from a variety of pine trees. They are small, white, teardrop-shaped sees that are rich and sweet.

PISTACHIO NUTS. Pistachio nuts are greenish-white nuts that are very sweet in flavor.

PUMPKIN SEEDS. Green, flat, and teardrop-shaped, pumpkin seeds make a great snack, and are great when sprinkled on salads.

SESAME SEEDS. Sesame seeds are tiny, off-white, tear-shaped seeds.

SUNFLOWER SEEDS. Sunflower seeds are pointed, gray, small seeds.

WALNUTS. Walnuts are round, flat, wavy nuts that are brown in color. They are rich in omega-3 fatty acids, which are reported to lower cholesterol levels.

NUT AND SEED BUTTERS

Nut and seed butters are the butters made from grinding nuts and seeds. They can be purchased in stores or made at home by grinding any raw nut or seed in a food processor. When buying nut butters in the store, make sure to read the label to ensure you are buying them raw, which means they contain only the nut or seed itself. In general, if the label doesn't specifically say "raw" or "untoasted," you can assume that the nut butter is toasted. The following list contains my favorite nut and seed butters that are commonly found in stores. Peanut butter is the only butter usually found in the supermarket. Almond, cashew, and tahini are usually available in health food stores. There are other, more obscure butters that you may have to order online (for information on how to do this, see the Resources section beginning on page 145).

ALMOND BUTTER. As its name implies, almond butter is butter that is derived from almonds. It is sweet and versatile, and a healthy substitute for peanut butter.

CASHEW BUTTER. Cashew butter is the butter derived from ground cashews. It is very sweet and creamy.

TAHINI. Tahini is butter made from ground sesame seeds. It is typical in Middle Eastern foods.

DRIED BEANS

Also known as "legumes," beans are packed with fiber and nutrients. In a raw food diet, dried beans are only consumed when sprouted, so that they are easily digested and the nutrients are easily assimilated into the body. When beans are sprouted, they are soaked and then rinsed with fresh water and drained a few times a day for several days, until they begin to grow sprouts. (For sprouting instructions, see page 30.)

ADZUKI BEANS. Adzuki beans are small, round, and have red skin. They are slightly sweet when sprouted.

GARBANZO BEANS. Also known as chickpeas, garbanzo beans are very easy to sprout. They are typical in Middle Eastern cuisine and have a nutty flavor.

KIDNEY BEANS. These beans get their name from their shape. They are red skinned and are somewhat neutral tasting when sprouted.

LENTILS. Lentils are small, flat, round beans that are very easily sprouted. Try experimenting with different varieties of lentils, as they are often available in red, green, or yellow.

PEAS. Green and round, peas are beans that are very sweet.

GRAINS

Grains are the kernels of a plant that produces a grass shoot. While abundant in a typical Western diet, the consumption of grains in a raw foods diet is limited, and usually consumed only when soaked or sprouted for maximum digestibility. The grains discussed in this section are those most common and appropriate for a raw food diet.

When purchasing grains, look for hulled, organic, whole grains in the bulk food section of your local health food store (not grains that have been partially processed).

AMARANTH. Amaranth is a grain that looks like tiny white circles. It is easy to sprout and is a great topping for salads.

CORN. Corn is a sweet grain that grows on tall plants called cobs. It can be consumed raw or sprouted. Many—including myself—prefer eating it right from the cob!

OAT GROATS. Oat groats are whole oat grains. They are available in bulk food bins and are easily digestible after they are germinated or soaked in water overnight.

QUINOA. Quinoa (pronounced *keen-wah*) is a grain that was once worshipped by the Aztecs. It is a tiny white circle and produces a sweet sprout.

RYE BERRIES. Rye berries are dark brown grains that are delicious when sprouted.

WHEAT. Wheat is a grass that is rich in chlorophyll. When shopping, look for wheat berries, which are simply the whole-wheat kernel. Wheat berries are easily sprouted and produce a sweet and chewy sprout.

CONDIMENTS

Condiments are additional, minimally-processed items that serve the purpose of adding flavor to your food. Most of the condiments at the supermarket contain lots of extra sugar and preservatives that can be unhealthy, are unwanted in a raw food diet, and are generally not necessary for the flavor. Below is a list of nutritious, pure condiments commonly used in raw food diets.

Bragg Liquid Aminos. Bragg is a sauce that is derived from soybeans. It contains amino acids and is very similar in taste to soy sauce.

Cacao. Cacao (pronounced *kuh-kah-oh*) is pure cocoa, or cocoa when the whole cocoa bean is intact. Originating in the Andes, cacao pods grow on small evergreen trees in the tropical regions. The cacao pod is the fruit of this tree and looks like a large green football. It contains twenty to sixty cocoa beans. These beans are used to make chocolate. When buying cocoa or cacao, make sure that the label says "raw" because if it doesn't, you can assume that the cocoa has been heated at high temperatures, destroying the precious enzymes. Cacao contains natural antioxidants—which can fight against cancer formation—and mood lifters. Keep in mind that historically, the terms "cocoa" and "cacao" have been used interchangeably to make things easier for the consumer. However, more accurately, cocoa is the processed powdered product, and cacao refers to the raw bean. There is such a thing as raw cocoa powder, but it is harder to find than cacao powder. To utilize food in a more pure form, simply make sure that whichever product you choose to buy is labeled as "raw."

Carob. Carob is a large, brown bean pod that has a chocolate, malt-like flavor. It is often used as a chocolate substitute because it contains no caffeine.

Kaffir Lime Leaves. Kaffir (pronounced *kah-fer*) lime leaves are leaves from a lime tree indigenous to Asia. They are used in Thai cooking and taste light and refreshing.

Miso. Miso is a soy paste that is aged and cultured. It is derived from rice and soybeans. Because of its fermentation, miso allows the nutritional properties of the soybeans to be easily assimilated into the body. Miso is rich in antioxidants and some studies suggest that the consumption of one bowl of miso soup per day can reduce the risk of developing breast cancer.

Red miso has been fermented for up to three years, and has a rich, earthy, salty taste.

White miso has a higher ratio of rice-to-soybeans, and the taste is mellow, sweet, and salty.

Nama Shoyu. Nama Shoyu is unpasteurized soy sauce. It has a rich, full-bodied flavor and is rich in enzymes and the healthful bacteria lactobacillus.

Nutritional Yeast. Nutritional yeast is flaky, yellow yeast that is grown off of beet sugars. It is completely different from the yeast that makes bread rise. Nutritional yeast is rich in vitamin B_{12}, which is often hard for vegetarians and raw foodies to get enough of. It has a slightly salty taste and is great sprinkled on salads, soups, or just about anything. Look for it in the bulk food section of your local health food store.

Oils. Oils should be purchased cold pressed and stored in the refrigerator. Oils are made by grinding nuts, seeds, or grains and then pressing them to release the oil (or applying pressure to the paste to extract the naturally occurring oils). When oils are marked "cold pressed" it means that no heat was applied when the oils were extracted. Raw oil contains the enzyme lipase that assists in the breakdown and digestion of the fats in oil and the fat in fat cells.

Coconut oil (also known as coconut butter) is extracted from the meat of a coconut. It is important to buy virgin (also called raw or unrefined) coconut oil, as its nutritional properties are very different from refined coconut oil. Although coconut oil does contain large amounts of saturated fats, when consumed in moderation and in its raw form, coconut oil can have a plethora of healing benefits (both antibacterial and antiviral) and huge immune-boosting properties. In addition to its healing benefits when it is consumed, coconut oil can be applied directly to the skin for a fantastic, pure lotion.

Flax oil is a nutty tasting oil derived from flax seeds. It has an abundance of the essential omega-3 and omega-6 fatty acids.

Hemp oil is oil derived from hemp seeds. It is nutty tasting and has the three-to-one ratio (three parts omega-6 to one part omega-3) of essential

SAMPLE SHOPPING LIST

Below is a typical shopping list for a well-stocked raw food kitchen. Although this list won't include all of the ingredients for every recipe, it does cover the basic main ingredients in many raw recipes.

FRUITS AND VEGETABLES

- Apples
- Avocados
- Bananas
- Beets
- Carrots
- Celery
- Chard
- Cilantro
- Ginger
- Kale
- Lemons
- Lettuce
- Oranges
- Parsley
- Pears
- Peas
- Spinach
- Tomatoes

DRIED FRUITS AND VEGETABLES

- Coconut flakes
- Dates
- Figs
- Mangos
- Raisins
- Sun-dried tomatoes

FRESH HERBS AND SPICES

- Basil
- Cilantro
- Garlic
- Ginger
- Oregano
- Thyme

OILS AND CONDIMENTS

- Apple Cider Vinegar
- Olive Oil (extra virgin)
- Miso
- Nama Shoyu
- Sea salt
- Vanilla extract (organic)

DRIED HERBS AND SPICES

- Cayenne pepper
- Chili powder
- Chipotle pepper
- Cinnamon
- Cumin
- Curry
- Oregano
- Smoked Spanish paprika

NUTS AND SEEDS

- Almonds
- Cashews
- Pine nuts
- Sesame seeds
- Sunflower seeds
- Walnuts

NUT AND SEED BUTTERS

- Almond butter
- Coconut oil or butter
- Dulse
- Nori
- Seaweed
- Tahini
- Wakame

SWEETENERS

- Dried fruits
- Raw honey

fatty acids that is optimal for the human body. Store hemp oil in the refrigerator and *do not ever* heat it, as it becomes toxic and unhealthy when heated.

Olive oil is oil derived form olives. Its taste varies form region to region.

Sesame oil is oil derived from sesame seeds. Be sure to look for unrefined, untoasted sesame oil. The flavor is nutty and sweet.

OLIVES. Olives are the fruits from an olive tree. They must be cured in brine before they are fit for consumption. Raw olives may be difficult to find (see the Resources section beginning on page 145 to find out where to get them). At the very least, buy olives that are in the refrigerated section of the store soaking in brine, as opposed to the canned variety, which are always cooked.

RICE WRAPPERS. Rice wrappers are thin, paper-like sheets that can be used to wrap vegetables, as you would do when making Sushi (page 100). They are made from rice flour, and although not technically considered "raw," they are considered to be "raw food friendly" since it is difficult to consume many of them in one sitting, and the ingredients are relatively pure.

TAMARI. Tamari is a brown sauce with a taste very similar to soy sauce. It is made from fermented soy beans and is slightly richer and darker than soy sauce.

VANILLA BEANS. Vanilla beans are the brown, thin, dried seedpod from a vanilla orchid. They are the origin of most all bottled vanilla flavorings. Vanilla beans are very expensive, but the flavor is superb. I usually use fresh vanilla beans for special occasions only. To consume, cut the bean in half lengthwise and scrape the tiny brown seeds out. One half of the inside of a vanilla bean equals about one tablespoon of vanilla extract.

VINEGAR. Vinegar, which means "sour wine," can be made from fermenting any fruit. When buying, look for a label that says "with the mother," which ensures that the vinegar is raw.

Apple cider vinegar is made from fermenting apples.

Balsamic vinegar is made from fermenting and aging grapes.

SWEETENERS

For a raw food diet, all sweeteners are derived from natural sources and are easily assimilated into the body. Keep in mind that dried fruits can also be used as sweeteners in many recipes.

AGAVE. Agave is a sweet syrup that is extracted from an agave plant (the same plant that is used to make tequila). Agave (also called agave nectar) is often used as a vegan substitute for honey, and has been called a healthy natural sweetener by many sources. However, recent reports have ignited controversy around agave, claiming that it is a highly processed sweetener, contrasting prior claims of agave's healthiness. Additionally, caution should be exercised when purchasing labels that say "raw." Some reports claim that since there are no laws regarding the labeling of raw food, simply seeing "raw" on a label does not necessarily mean the product in question is raw—it may mean that the product comes from a raw material, but has still been heated at over 118°F during processing and/or has been highly processed from its original form. Because agave may potentially be heated above 118°F and because of the processing involved in making agave syrup, I would recommend staying away from agave. Raw honey or dried fruits can be used in its place, which is what I have done for all the recipes in this book.

HONEY. Honey is sweet syrup produced by honeybees. Worker bees collect nectar from flowers and convert the nectar into honey in the hive. The honey is then stored in combs to be used as a food source if needed. The flavor of honey varies greatly depending on the types of flowers the bees collect nectar from. For example, orange blossom honey is produced from orange blossom flowers, and has a very different flavor than lavender honey, which is produced from lavender flowers. I encourage you to experiment with different varieties. If you are lucky enough to find honey that is produced locally, it is known to aid in allergy relief, as it exposes and desensitizes the body to safe amounts of locally-grown flowers and their pollens. Although honey can be purchased in many forms, for the purposes of a raw food diet (and optimal nutrition) I recommend buying honey that is either labeled as "raw" or still in the comb. Read the labels on honey carefully, because unless they specifically state that the honey is unheated and raw, you can safely assume the honey has been heated and processed. (It is important to note that the FDA does not recommend raw honey for infants, the elderly, pregnant women, or anyone with a compromised immune system.)

Comb honey is made up of raw, pure honey sections taken straight from the hive with very minimal processing. Although this type of honey has a rougher texture, it contains the added benefits of being the least processed. Bees fill the hexagon-shaped wax cells of the comb with honey and cap it with beeswax. Honeycomb is similar to a chewy candy when it is consumed.

Raw honey is rich in enzymes, aids in digestion, and is high in antioxidants. Raw honey looks milkier and creamier than heated honey and it contains particles of bee pollen (an antibacterial) and propolis (a natural antibiotic, rich in amino acids and immune-boosting properties).

STEVIA. Stevia is a powdered sweetener derived from an herb. It is reported to be 100 times as sweet as sugar.

GROWING YOUR OWN KITCHEN GARDEN

Rather than purchasing herbs and sprouts, many raw foodies choose to grow their own, creating a kitchen garden. This is often an easy and cost-efficient endeavor that brings the joy and flavors of fresh herbs to the preparation of each meal.

Growing your own container kitchen garden can be a completely inspiring and exciting endeavor. The first time I grew a container garden in my kitchen I was amazed at how easy it was. Depending on the amount of space and the energy level that you have, a container garden can be as simple as one big pot containing several fresh herbs, or a more elaborate set of pots containing plants that are companions and grow well together.

Adding a few tablespoons of freshly picked herbs can make a meal go from just delicious to absolutely memorable—especially for you, the chef, when you know the herbs were grown and picked in your own kitchen. (See the Resources section beginning on page 145 to learn where you can purchase indoor gardening supplies and equipment.)

Starting a container kitchen garden is easy if you follow these steps. (For additional tips, see the inset on page 32.)

1. Select your containers. Make sure they are deep enough to hold plants in. Keep in mind that plants need to have room for their roots to grow. In general, salad greens and basil can grow well in containers that are four to five inches deep, while most other plants will be fine in containers that are twelve inches deep.

   When choosing your containers, consider the following:

   • Material. Containers should be made from

non-toxic materials, such as non-treated wood, bamboo, or willow.

● Proper space for the plants when they are fully grown. You can usually figure out how big the plant will be when fully grown by reading the seed package. The package should also tell you how much space to allow between each plant.

● Proper drainage. Be sure to select containers with small holes in the bottom that allow excess water to drain out into a holding tray.

2. Choose a location for the plants—either indoors or outside. If you are growing plants outside, the climate will determine which kinds of plants can be grown during which season. In general, root crops and greens can get by with indirect sunlight (through a window or in a shaded spot), but fruiting plants require full, direct sunlight for at least six to eight hours a day.

The table on page 31, adapted from Indoor Gardening Supplies, provides information about the optimal conditions and climates for growing your own garden, both indoors and outside. For the plants that require supplemental lighting, see the Resources section (beginning on page 145) for information on where to order these lights.

SPROUTS

Growing your own sprouts is one of the easiest, healthiest things you can learn to do. To sprout seeds, you simply soak them in water, then drain and rinse for several days in a strainer or colander until they grow little sprouts. There is no soil involved. When seeds, legumes, and grains are sprouted, their nutritional content is increased tremendously, making them far easier to digest. In addition, sprouting is one of the most economical ways that we can feed our bodies. For example, it will likely cost less than a quarter to buy about $1/4$ cup of dried lentils. When sprouted, these will yield about one cup of lentil sprouts. These sprouts will provide you with roughly 7 grams of protein, 21 percent of your daily allowance for vitamin C, and 14 percent of your daily allowance for iron. Sprinkling one cup of sprouts on any salad in this book is a great way to add flavor and nutrition to a meal—and not break the bank while doing so!

The easiest way to sprout is by using a colander. It doesn't require you to buy any special equipment and it is pretty straightforward. In general, there are only five steps you should follow.

1. Soak the seeds in cool water. In general, most seeds should be soaked overnight or for 12 hours but some require less soaking time. The table on page 34 lists the appropriate soaking times for common seeds. (If the seed isn't listed, soaking it for 12 hours will be appropriate.)

2. Transfer the soaked seeds to a colander. Rinse well with cool water.

3. Drain the seeds. It is easiest to leave the colander in the sink, if you have the room. Otherwise, place the colander on a counter or other surface with paper towels or a towel under it to absorb excess moisture.

4. Cover the colander loosely. A plate or a piece of paper towel both work just fine.

5. Rinse and drain the seeds (re-covering the colander after every draining) twice a day for several days until the sprouts have reached the same length as the grain or seed itself (usually

Basics for Growing a Kitchen Garden

Plant	Conditions for Indoor Growth	Optimal Climate for Outdoor Growth	Difficulty	Considerations
Basil	Sunny windowsill	All	Easy	Does best in direct sunlight.
Chives	Sunny windowsill	All	Easy	
Lettuce	Sunny windowsill	Cooler to mild climates	Easy	In colder climates, use supplemental fluorescent lights to grow indoors.
Mint	Sunny windowsill	All	Easy	
Parsley	Sunny windowsill	All	Easy	
Rosemary	Sunny windowsill	Dry	Moderate	Sensitive to proper drainage and good air circulation indoors (can get moldy if air indoors is too humid). Needs direct sunlight.
Spinach	Sunny windowsill	Cooler to mild climates	Moderate	In colder climates, use supplemental fluorescent lights to grow indoors.
Thyme	Sunny windowsill	All	Easy	
Tomatoes	Warm, sunny windowsill	Warm	Moderate	Requires warm temperatures and supplemental lights to be grown indoors.

between $1/4$ inch and 1 inch long). This is when the sprouts are typically the most nutritious, and therefore it is the optimal time for consumption.

6. Refrigerate. Once the seeds have sprouted, wrap them in a dry piece of paper towel and transfer them to the refrigerator.

That's it! Once refrigerated, the sprouts will last about four days to one week. If they look questionable, toss them—better to be safe than sorry!

There are other ways to sprout that require equipment, but using a colander is by far the easiest way. If you don't have the room for a colander to

TIPS FOR GROWING
AN INDOOR KITCHEN GARDEN

If you live in a colder climate, consider growing an indoor container garden. People who live in warmer climates can grow gardens indoors too, but it is especially beneficial for those living in colder climates, which can prevent crops from properly growing outside.

The following tips will help you, should you decide to grow an indoor kitchen garden.

1. A big, south-facing, sunny window is the best place to put your containers, as your plants will all be craving the sun.

2. A great place to start, in almost all climates, is by growing a variety of fresh herbs. These can be a tremendous addition to any raw food recipe in this book. Some of my favorites that can be grown indoors year-round include basil, cilantro, rosemary, chives, mint, thyme, spinach, dill, and parsley. Small tomatoes and some lettuces are usually great for indoor gardens as well. Larger tomatoes, however, will require some supplemental growing lights.

3. Pay special attention to preventing bugs from getting in your indoor containers—this will help ensure that your plants are healthy and happy. The best way to protect from bugs is to keep your plants healthy by providing adequate light, water, and drainage. That being said, indoor gardens can be susceptible to insects as there is no cold weather to kill them off. If you do find eggs or bugs on your indoor plants, an easy method of killing and removing them is to prepare some warm, soapy water (1 teaspoon natural, biodegradable soap and 2 cups water) and place it in a spray bottle. Spray the soapy water on the infected plants until they are dripping wet, being sure to spray the undersides of the leaves as well (this is where the bugs usually hang out). After an hour or two, repeat these steps with a clean water spray. Once the bugs are gone and the soapy residue is sprayed off, your plants will be safe to eat.

4. Start with rich, organic potting soil. It is important that this soil is light so that it drains properly. "Soilless" mixes, such as container sit in your sink for a few days, consider buying a sprouting bag. For relatively cheap, you can buy a mold-resistant hemp bag that can hang off your faucet. The bags can be reused over and over again, as long as they are washed in between uses. The steps for using the bag are the same as a colander: soak, rinse, and drain; the seeds simply stay in the bag until they are fully sprouted.

(See the Resources section beginning on page 145 for information on ordering these bags.)

Most seeds, grains, and legumes are candidates for sprouting. However, each seed and grain takes a different amount of time to reach its maximum nutritional value. The table on page 34 lists general soaking and sprouting times for some common seeds and grains, most of which tend to mixes or transplant mixes, work best. Combine a small amount of pesticide-free organic compost, which is topsoil produced from broken-down organic matter, and mix this in the soil as well. This will pack lots of nutrients into your garden.

5. Fertilize! Fertilizing plants in containers is very important, as your plants are confined to a tiny box and are not getting nutrients from outdoor soil that has been sowed over for many years. Consider adding a small amount of organic fertilizer to the soil before planting, and then use an additional water-soluble organic fertilizer once a week to help boost the plants' nutrients.

6. Plant seeds the same distance apart as you would in a traditional garden. If your containers are very small, put a few small plants in a pot, or one average-sized plant per pot. Additionally, consider planting companion plants together. Companion plants are plants that have beneficial relationships when you plant them next to each other, such as greater evidence of pest control, pollination, and crop productivity. The following list contains some of these popular companion plants that do well together.

- Lettuce and herbs
- Carrots and beans
- Tomatoes and basil

7. Water your plants. It is imperative you pay special attention to the watering needs of your plants—especially for indoor gardens. Because the volume of soil is relatively low, it is easier for the plants to dry out. You may need to water once or even twice a day, depending on the plants' locations. You should add water until it starts to come out of the drainage hole, but stop before the soil becomes very soggy.

8. Consider the state-of-the-art resources available. Many technologies are now available to aid in container gardens. One of these high-tech devices that is worth mentioning is Aerogrow. Aerogrow is a planting device that uses NASA technology to grow plants in water—no soil is necessary. It fits onto your countertop and yields an amazing amount of produce in a small space indoors. Aerogrow is an amazing tool for an indoor garden—you may want to invest in one. See the Resources section (beginning on page 145) for ordering information.

be very easy to sprout and will present very few complications.

When buying grains and legumes, always try to find organic ones. Because you are getting a concentrated amount of nutrients in these little seeds once you sprout them, buying seeds that are organic will ensure that you won't be consuming unnecessary and unhealthy pesticide residues at the same time. Organic seeds are very common and easy to find in most health food stores. However, I have found the most success when ordering these seeds from companies that test them to make sure that they are viable batches for sprouting. To find out where to order seeds, see the Resources section (beginning on page 145).

Basic Sprouting Information

Seed, Legume, or Grain	Starting Amount	Soaking Time	Sprouting Time	Approximate Yield
Alfalfa	3 tablespoons	8 hours	4 to 6 days	3 cups
Beans, adzuki	1 cup	12 hours	3 days	4 cups
Beans, garbanzo	1 cup	12 hours	2 to 3 days	3 cups
Broccoli	3 tablespoons	8 hours	3 to 4 days	3 cups
Buckwheat, hulled	1 cup	12 hours	2 to 3 days	3 cups
Lentils, red	1 cup	12 hours	2 to 3 days	3 cups
Peas	1 cup	12 hours	2 to 3 days	2 cups
Quinoa	1 cup	12 hours	2 days	2 cups
Radish	3 tablespoons	8 hours	3 days	3 cups
Wheat, soft	1 cup	12 hours	2 days	2 cups

ORGANIZATION

It is a lot easier (and more fun) to prepare raw meals when your kitchen is organized in a raw food-friendly way. Here are some helpful tips for organizing your kitchen:

- Acquire at least ten sealable glass jars of varying sizes for all of the bulk ingredients that you will be purchasing. Set aside a spot in your pantry where all of the bulk ingredients can be stored and are easily accessible. Nothing is more frustrating and time-wasting than rifling through a drawer of plastic bags filled with unidentifiable bulk foods.

- Plan on food shopping at least twice a week. The amount of produce that you go through will be surprising at first. Unless you have an enormous refrigerator, it is hard to store that much produce.

- Invest in a few good-quality containers to store your leftovers. While food is always best when served fresh, if your whole family isn't eating this way, it is helpful to prepare and store some recipes in advance. If possible, look for glass containers with plastic lids—some containers

GETTING YOUR KIDS INVOLVED

Involving your kids in the preparation of foods will help them get excited about eating healthier. If they help make it, they will probably be more excited to eat it. Of course, this also promotes family time, and sharing healthy food is a great way to enjoy your family and teach habits that will last a lifetime.

• Kids usually love to help make anything that involves the food processor or blender. Little ones will be excited to add things to the food processor in recipes like Mango Soup (page 111) and Pesto (page 56).

• The desserts are always a hit with kids. Even if it's hard to get kids to eat their greens, they will at least be getting great nutrients from these raw desserts. Involve kids in making these desserts. They will delight that they can lick the bowl to their hearts content, and you will delight that that they can do so with no worries of raw eggs or stomachaches from too much processed food.

• Many of the recipes in this book are friendly for little fingers, as they don't involve sharp tools or heat. Try getting kids to help with rolling Spring Rolls (page 96), forming the crust into the pan for Banana Mango Cream Pie (page 122), or layering the Baklava (page 91).

• Use cookie cutters even if you aren't making cookies. Your children will love to cut vegetables into fun shapes as in Daikon Dumplings (page 103) or "Ceviche" (page 135).

• Involve children in the preparation and growing of your kitchen garden (see page 29). Involving kids in growing the food is a fantastic way to get them interested in how it tastes.

made up of all plastic have been known to give off gases that are unhealthy.

• Consider starting a raw food club of friends that are interested in a healthier lifestyle. It is so much fun and so inspiring to have monthly raw food potlucks, and if everyone chips in to share the costs of buying items in bulk, you'll save money too.

• Get the whole family involved! If possible, include your family in the preparation of these meals. If you all are excited about the beautiful and fresh ingredients, it's more fun. See the inset above for helpful ideas on getting your kids involved.

PRESENTATION

Raw food, when prepared successfully, can ignite an explosion of culinary senses. On the other hand, raw food prepared unsuccessfully can be unappealing and uninviting to consume. It is all in how you present the final product.

After preparing raw food for many years, I have developed some tricks of the trade that can help turn your creations into true masterpieces. If you follow these guidelines, your food will look fantastic and your family and friends will be begging for more!

GENERAL GUIDELINES

The following guidelines are not recipe-specific. Following these tips will ensure your creations look—and taste!—as wonderful and appetizing as possible.

- It's all about texture. A large part of successful raw food preparation is the texture of the final product. Because so much of the food is blended and combined in ways our taste buds and eyes may not be used to, it is important that the texture of the food imitates what one might expect. For example, when preparing a raw food hummus dip that includes carrots, if the final product were to have chunks of crunchy carrots in it, the diner might find that odd, and as a result, unappealing. Or, if the crust of a delicate pine nut tart is chunky and gritty instead of light and smooth, the tart might not be perceived as heavenly as it could be. Conversely, if the hummus is creamy and smooth and the pine nut crust is light and flaky, the overall dining experience will be much more pleasing and delightful. A suitable-textured end product can, for the most part, be easily achieved by first blending together the harder-textured items in any recipe (unless specified otherwise) and then continuing with the recipe. For the recipes in this book, I have followed this rule. For example, chopping the nuts completely before adding the honey in the Honey Pine Nut Tart crust (page 59) will ensure a smooth and light texture. Additionally, coarsely chopping the carrots before adding them to the food processor and blending with the other ingredients will ensure a light and creamy Hummus (page 79).

- Try to avoid presenting food that is all one color. For example, if you are preparing a blended soup and it turns out to be bright red, it is important to add color and interest to the red soup with a garnish of another color (as in the Chilled Avocado Tomato Soup, page 63). Garnishes, which are edible decorations, have long been used in traditional French and fine cooking, and are a great way to add color and interest to any dish. Eating food that looks beautiful tells our minds and our bodies that it will taste beautiful as well. Easy garnishes that add color include chopped parsley, finely-diced tomatoes, a sprinkling of olives or capers, grated carrots, or even a dusting of paprika.

- Consider gently warming food in the dehydrator or over a very low flame on the stovetop before serving. If you are serving a dish that would traditionally be eaten warm, it might not taste as fantastic if presented cold. Consider warming gently (without destroying the enzymes) over a low flame, or even just warming the serving plates in the oven before plating the food.

- If serving more than one dish on a plate, imagine dividing the plate into thirds (as if you were cutting a pie into three equal wedges) and arranging one dish on each third of the plate. When presenting plates to guests, the "main course" should always be on the third that is closest to the person.

- Have fun and get creative with shapes. You don't need to be a master chef in order to make simple, fun shapes out of vegetables to add as garnishees to your dishes. Your guests will delight in the presentation of something as simple as a star shape cut out of a red bell pepper. Fun shapes can turn ordinary meals into very memorable experiences. Try experimenting with cookie cutters to make different shapes out of thinly-sliced vegetables. Fan thin slices of a vegetable (such as carrots) around the outside of a plate for a spectacular decoration. Drizzle olive oil in a circular pattern around the outside rim of a plate. Make a "mountain" of shredded carrots that sits in the middle of a beautiful green salad. Have fun!

SALAD GUIDELINES

Following these guidelines will ensure your raw food salads not only taste great, but look great as well.

- Keep the salad off the rim of the plate. Think of the rim as a picture frame and the salad as the picture.

- Aim for a good mix of colors. Garnishing with different fruits or vegetables can help with this.

- Adding height to a salad makes it look more appealing.

- Cut the ingredients neatly and into bite-sized pieces.

SOUP GUIDELINES

Following these guidelines will ensure your raw food soups not only taste great, but look great as well.

- Wait until just before serving to add the toppings to any soup. This keeps the ingredients from getting soggy.

- Consider using a garnish or topping that is an ingredient in the soup itself. For example, if you were making a blended tomato soup with cucumbers, consider carefully cutting a few slices of cucumber and placing them on the soup as a garnish just before serving.

- A very elegant way of serving soup and toppings at a dinner party is to place a spoonful of the topping in each bowl first, and then ladle the soup directly over the topping. The end result may look the same once in the bowl, but if you do this at the table while your guests are seated and watching, it appears elegant and is a very beautiful and visually striking way of serving the soup. This is the way soup is usually presented in very fine French restaurants.

DESSERT GUIDELINES

Following these guidelines will ensure your raw food desserts not only taste great, but look great as well.

- Traditionally, desserts are presented on a plate with three elements in mind: the dessert itself, the garnish, and the sauce. Certainly you don't need to do this every time in order for a dessert to be appealing, but consider how delightful a pine nut tart becomes if served with some cashew cream and drizzled with raw honey.

- Keep in mind the color, shape, and flavor of what you add to a plated dessert. Visually, a variety of colors can be pleasing, but be careful not to make too much of a rainbow of colors.

- Shaving dark chocolate (make sure it is at least 70 percent dark or raw) with a vegetable peeler over any dessert gives it a very sophisticated look.

- A cluster of fresh mint leaves and/or a decorative drizzle of honey is a beautiful garnish on most dessert plates.

CONCLUSION

This chapter was designed to provide you with everything you need to know if you are interested in starting a raw food diet. While embarking on something so different and new can be intimidating and scary, I hope that this chapter has helped you gain confidence and assure you that if you set your mind to it, you can succeed on your raw food diet.

Additionally, growing your own garden and sprouts can be some of the most rewarding and inspirational experiences for experienced raw foodies and novices alike. The sprouts are phenomenally nutritious, and it's fun to watch them grow. In addition, growing your own sprouts can cost just a few pennies, as compared to the expensive sprouts sold in local stores. Other cost-effective ways to enhance your raw food experience include properly organizing your kitchen, which will eliminate the stress from unnecessary clutter; getting your kids involved, which will ensure the whole family has fun while eating healthy; and presenting your creations in a visually-pleasing manner. The tips and guidelines in this chapter can help you achieve all of this.

So don't be afraid to experiment and have fun with the process—this is an exciting time in your life. Enjoy it!

2

Italian Raw Cuisine

After spending several summers traveling in Italy, I became determined to recreate my favorite Italian dishes so that they would be as healthy as they were delicious. The recipes in this chapter—which include soups, appetizers, snacks, salads, dressings, meals, marinades, and desserts—are the result of my experimental time spent in the kitchen, trying to create an array of simple, raw Italian recipes. I think that the recipes I have chosen for this chapter are wildly successful at combining delicious flavor with wonderful, healthy ingredients. All of the recipes have been taste-tested by myself, my family, and my friends, and each and every one has received a seal of approval—from raw foodies and non-raw foodies alike!

It doesn't matter if you are just starting on your raw food journey or if you have been eating raw for some time—if you enjoy Italian cuisine, this chapter will contain a recipe for you. Be sure to check out the Menu Ideas section on the next page, which includes ideas for both simple and elegant Italian feasts that will bring the exquisite flavors of Italy right to your kitchen.

Menu Ideas

Having simple, ready-to-use menu ideas can help you plan your next Italian meal effortlessly and seamlessly. The sample menus below highlight particular flavor pairings that enhance one another for each course of the meal. In addition, I have included options for either a simple, quick meal or an elaborate feast that takes more time to prepare. Knowing in advance the amount of time a meal will take to prepare can take the guesswork out of raw food preparation, which often requires a bit of advance planning.

A Simple and Quick Italian Meal
(Prepare right before serving)

Butternut Squash Soup with Walnut Tapenade

Zucchini "Fettuccine"

Strawberries with Balsamic Glaze
and Whipped Cream

An Elegant Feast
(Requires extra time and equipment)

Radicchio Bruschetta
(requires 1 hour to marinate)

Tomato, Pesto, Basil, and Cashew "Cheese" Terrines
(make ahead in the morning)

Chocolate Cherry Biscotti
(begin 12 hours ahead to dehydrate)

Radicchio Bruschetta

This bruschetta is such a beautiful array of colors and fresh tastes, you'll never miss the bread!

1. Place all of the ingredients except the radicchio in a large bowl and mix well. Let marinate for 1 hour at room temperature.

2. Scoop a heaping tablespoon of the tomato mixture onto each radicchio leaf and serve.

FOR A CHANGE . . .

● Use romaine lettuce instead of radicchio leaves.

● Top each serving of bruschetta with a teaspoon of Pesto (page 56).

● Sprinkle some chopped scallions and/or diced avocados over each serving.

Yield: 8 to 10 servings

2 cloves garlic, chopped

4 cups quartered cherry tomatoes

1 cup chopped fresh basil

4 tablespoons freshly squeezed lemon juice

1 tablespoon cold pressed extra virgin olive oil

1 teaspoon sea salt

8 to 10 large radicchio leaves

TIP . . .

In order to minimize seeds in your freshly squeezed lemon juice, cut each lemon in half width-wise. Hold the lemon over a bowl with the cut side facing up and squeeze. This way, most of the seeds will remain inside the lemon instead of falling into the bowl with the juice.

Vegetables Marinated in Oil and Lemon

In Italy, there is an age-old tradition of marinating vegetables to make the most of the plentiful harvest. This recipe needs to be made several days before it is served, but it is well worth the wait.

Yield: 6 to 8 servings

• • • • • • •

1 red bell pepper, sliced into long, thin strips

1 pound baby portabella mushroom caps, wiped clean and sliced

1 cup Basic Italian Marinade (page 54)

$1/4$ cup pearl onions, peeled and halved

1. Place all the ingredients in a large bowl and mix well. Cover and refrigerate 2 to 3 days.

2. Remove the vegetables from the refrigerator and let sit for 2 hours. Serve at room temperature.

FOR A CHANGE . . .

● Add some diced avocados to the marinated vegetables right before serving. Halve 4 avocados, scoop out the flesh, and cut into $1/2$-inch cubes. Add the cubes to the vegetables and mix gently. Scoop the vegetable mixture into the empty avocado shells and serve.

● Add 1 teaspoon of your favorite dried herb to the marinade for a different flavor, such as herbes de Provence, rosemary, or sage.

Butternut Squash Soup with Sage and Walnut Tapenade

The flavor of this soup is so superb, one taste will transport you to the Northern Italian countryside. Steaming the squash allows for it to be more easily digested (especially for those new to raw food or with weakened digestive systems), while still preserving most of the nutrients. I prefer using flat Italian parsley for the tapenade, but the curly variety can be used as well.

1. Place the shallot, squash, onion, and salt in a large soup pot and add water until the vegetables are just covered. Bring to a simmer, then cook 5 to 7 minutes, just until the squash is tender when pierced with a fork. Reserving the cooking water, drain the vegetables and set aside.

2. To make the tapenade, place the walnuts, parsley, sage, and salt in a food processor and blend until the mixture appears smooth, but a little coarse. Transfer the mixture to a small mixing bowl, add the tomatoes and olive oil, and gently combine by hand. Set aside.

3. Transfer the squash mixture to a food processor. Add the honey and cinnamon and process until smooth, adding just enough of the reserved cooking water to reach the desired soup consistency.

4. Ladle the soup into bowls, top with 1 to 2 tablespoons of tapenade, and serve.

Yield: 6 to 8 servings

I shallot, coarsely chopped

4 cups peeled, seeded, and cubed butternut squash

I cup coarsely chopped sweet onion, preferably Vidalia

1 1/2 teaspoons sea salt

2 tablespoons raw honey

1/8 teaspoon cinnamon

Tapenade

1/3 cup finely chopped raw or untoasted walnuts

1/4 cup finely chopped fresh parsley

1 1/2 teaspoons chopped fresh sage

1/2 teaspoon sea salt

1/2 cup diced tomatoes

6 tablespoons cold pressed extra virgin olive oil

Rustic Tomato Salad

Of all the amazing salads and fantastic creations I have eaten in Italy, this simple tomato salad is by far my favorite. It really pays to buy the best ingredients for this recipe, as the taste will be extraordinary. In Italy, this salad is typically served on a piece of crostini or lightly toasted bread. Adapted to meet a raw cuisine standard, it is served in lightly marinated mushroom caps. I think I like this version even better than the original!

Yield: 6 servings

. . . .

6 large portabella mushroom caps, wiped clean

2 tablespoons balsamic vinegar

4 cups halved red grape tomatoes

4 cups halved yellow grape tomatoes

$^1/_3$ cup coarsely chopped fresh basil

$^1/_2$ cup Best Basic Italian Dressing (page 48)

1. Place the mushroom caps gill-side up on a large, shallow plate. Drizzle with the vinegar and set aside.

2. Place all of the remaining ingredients in a medium bowl and mix well. Let marinate for 15 minutes at room temperature.

3. Spoon the tomato mixture onto the mushroom caps and serve.

FOR A CHANGE . . .

● Add $^1/_2$ cup chopped kalamata olives to the salad ingredients before letting them marinate.

● Sprinkle 2 tablespoons capers over the filled mushroom caps.

● Use all red or all yellow grape tomatoes instead of combining the two.

FYI . . .

One medium tomato provides up to 40 percent of the Recommended Daily Allowance (RDA) of vitamin C!

Sicilian Salad

This is my version of a typical Sicilian salad. The sweet oranges contrast perfectly with the earthy olives, spicy red onion, and peppery arugula greens. For best results, use blood oranges and baby arugula.

Yield: 6 to 8 servings

2 oranges, peeled and cut into $1/2$ inch slices

$1/2$ red onion, cut into very thin rings

$1/2$ cup Sweet Sicilian Dressing (page 49)

4 cups loosely packed arugula

$1/2$ cup pitted kalamata olives

$1/2$ cup lightly crushed raw or untoasted walnuts

1. Place the oranges, onion, and dressing in a medium bowl and toss together. Let marinate for 15 minutes at room temperature.

2. Place the arugula in a large salad bowl. Add the orange-onion mixture and gently toss.

3. Scatter the olives and walnuts on top of the salad and serve immediately.

FOR A CHANGE . . .

● Substitute red or pink grapefruits for the oranges.

● Add $1/2$ cup crushed raw or untoasted pistachio nuts to the finished salad before serving.

TIP . . .

To store the arugula, wash and dry it and wrap it in a paper towel before placing in an airtight bag in the fridge. It will last longer this way.

Fennel and Orange Salad With Honey-Walnut Topping

Yield: 4 to 5 servings

2 clementine oranges

4 radishes, cut into
small cubes

I fennel bulb, halved and cut
into small cubes

I avocado, cut into $1/2$-inch cubes

$1/2$ red bell pepper,
cut into small cubes

$1/2$ cup chopped fresh Italian
parsley

$1/2$ cup Best Basic Italian
Dressing (page 48)

10 to 12 Belgian endive leaves

Honey-Walnut Topping

$1/4$ cup coarsely chopped raw
or untoasted walnuts

I tablespoon raw honey

I tablespoon freshly squeezed
lemon juice

*Belgian endive leaves double as edible bowls for
this exquisite-tasting, visually beautiful salad.
This is the perfect starter course for a special meal.*

1. To make the topping, place the walnuts, honey, and lemon juice in a small bowl and mix well. Set aside.

2. Peel the clementines and separate the sections. Cut each section in half or thirds (depending on their size) and place in a large bowl along with the radishes, fennel, avocado, bell pepper, and parsley. Add the dressing and mix well.

3. Arrange the endive leaves on a serving platter. Fill each leaf with orange-fennel mixture, top with some honey-walnut topping, and serve.

FOR A CHANGE . . .

● Peel and cut a navel or juice orange into bite-size pieces and use instead of the clementines.

Tomato, Pesto, Basil, and Cashew "Cheese" Terrines

Prepared in standard muffin cups, these terrines are absolutely gorgeous—and perfect to serve as appetizers or light entrées. They may take a little effort to prepare, but the results are worth it. When buying tomatoes for this dish, look for any heirloom variety that is about three inches in diameter (the same circumference as the muffin cups).

1. Combine the garlic, basil, olive oil, lemon juice, and salt in a medium bowl. Let marinate for 15 minutes at room temperature.

2. In a separate bowl, combine the Cashew "Cheese" and the rosemary and mix well. Set aside.

3. Line 6 cups of a standard 3-inch muffin tin with plastic wrap (leave extra around the edges for easy removal of the terrines). In each cup, layer the ingredients in the following order: 1 tomato slice, 1 tablespoon Cashew Cheese, 1 tablespoon Sun-Dried Tomato Pesto, 1 tablespoon marinated basil, and end with another tomato slice. Refrigerate for at least 1 hour to set.

3. Just before serving, place the mixed greens in a large salad bowl, add the dressing, and toss. Mound about 1 cup of the greens on 6 individual salad plates and set aside.

4. To remove the terrines, place a baking sheet on top of the muffin tin and flip it over. Remove the plastic wrap.

5. Using a spatula, remove the terrines from the baking sheet and place one on top of each mound of greens. Serve immediately.

FOR A CHANGE . . .

● Add ¼ cup chopped kalamata olives, a handful of crushed raw or untoasted pistachios or almonds, 1 teaspoon nutritional yeast, and/or a handful of raw pine nuts to the greens before placing the terrines on top.

Yield: 6 terrines

● ● ● ● ● ● ●

½ clove garlic, finely minced

½ cup chopped fresh basil

1 tablespoon cold pressed extra virgin olive oil

½ tablespoon freshly squeezed lemon juice

¼ teaspoon sea salt

½ cup Cashew "Cheese" (page 53)

1 tablespoon chopped fresh rosemary

3 large tomatoes, cut into 12 slices

½ cup Sun-Dried Tomato Pesto (page 56)

6 cups mixed baby greens

¼ cup Best Basic Italian Dressing (page 48)

Best Basic Italian Dressing

*This dressing is so pure and so simple to make,
you may never want to go back to
the bottled variety!*

Yield: About 1 cup

2 cloves garlic, finely minced

1 shallot, finely minced

$\frac{1}{2}$ cup freshly squeezed lemon juice

2 teaspoons finely chopped fresh oregano

1 $\frac{1}{2}$ teaspoons sea salt

$\frac{1}{2}$ teaspoon freshly ground black pepper

$\frac{1}{2}$ cup cold pressed extra virgin olive oil

1. Place all the ingredients except the olive oil in a jar with a lid (a Mason jar is good). Cover, shake well, and let sit for 15 minutes at room temperature.

2. Add the olive oil to jar, cover, and shake vigorously until the ingredients are well combined.

3. Use the dressing immediately, or refrigerate until ready to use. If refrigerating, allow the dressing to return to room temperature and stir vigorously before using.

FYI . . .

Leftover jam jars are perfect for making and storing dressings—and reusing them is a great way to recycle!

Creamy Italian Dressing

This creamy, flavorful dressing goes well with any salad.

1. Place the pine nuts in a food processor and pulse until smooth. Add all the remaining ingredients and blend until completely incorporated.

2. Use the dressing immediately or place in a covered container and refrigerate until ready to use. If refrigerating, allow the dressing to return to room temperature and stir vigorously before using.

Yield: About 1 cup

1/4 cup raw or untoasted pine nuts

2 cloves garlic

1/2 cup cold pressed extra virgin olive oil

1/2 cup freshly squeezed lemon juice

2 tablespoons apple cider vinegar

1 tablespoon Bragg Liquid Aminos or tamari soy sauce

2 teaspoons chopped fresh oregano

2 teaspoons chopped fresh Italian parsley

1 teaspoon chopped fresh thyme

FYI . . .

When blended, pine nuts and cashews have a creamier consistency than other nuts.

Sweet Sicilian Dressing

This sweet and spicy dressing is fantastic on salads, particularly ones that contain fruit.

1. Place all of the ingredients in a food processor and pulse until completely incorporated.

2. Use the dressing immediately, or place in a covered container and refrigerate until ready to use. If refrigerating, allow the dressing to return to room temperature and stir vigorously before using.

Yield: About 1 cup

1/2 cup freshly squeezed lemon juice

1/2 cup cold pressed extra virgin olive oil

1 tablespoon raw honey

1/2 teaspoon sea salt

1/8 teaspoon ground cumin

TASTES GREAT WITH . . .

Sicilian Salad (page 45) or Spinach Salad with Jicama and Pineapple (page 114).

Zucchini "Fettuccine"

In this recipe, zucchini is transformed into "fettuccine noodles"
and then topped with flavorful marinara sauce.
It is a delicious alternative to pasta.

Yield: 3 to 4 servings

• • • • • • •

3 medium zucchini

4 cups Marinara Sauce
(page 55)

1. Peel the zucchini, then cut them into pieces about $2\frac{1}{2}$ inches long.

2. Using a spiralizer (see page 9 for directions) or a vegetable peeler (see FYI below), cut each piece of zucchini into long flat "noodles." Place the noodles in a colander or strainer and let sit for 20 minutes at room temperature to release excess moisture. This prevents the sauce from getting watery when you add it.

3. Transfer the noodles to a serving bowl, toss with the sauce, and serve immediately.

FOR A CHANGE . . .

• Instead of (or in addition to) zucchini, make the noodles with another firm, round vegetable. Beets, butternut squash, jicama, and summer squash are good choices.

• Instead of marinara, toss the noodles with Pesto (page 56) or simply add a drizzle of olive oil, some chopped tomatoes, a little fresh basil, and a sprinkling of sea salt.

FYI . . .

If you don't own a spiralizer, you can use a vegetable peeler to make long, flat noodles. To do this, peel the vegetable and hold it in one hand. With your other hand, take the vegetable peeler and press down on the vegetable. Slowly move the peeler from the top of the vegetable to the bottom, using long, sweeping strokes to cut thin, flat strips.

"Orzo" with Arugula Peas, and Tomatoes

This is a raw version of a classic Italian dish that is traditionally made with orzo pasta. It combines sprouted wheat berries with sweet peas and tomatoes. The sweet peas contrast beautifully with the sharp, peppery taste of arugula, and this dish couldn't be simpler to prepare.

1. Place all of the ingredients in a large bowl and mix well.

2. Transfer the mixture to plates and serve immediately.

FOR A CHANGE . . .

● For a creamier version of this dish, add $\frac{1}{2}$ cup Cashew "Cheese" (page 53).

Yield: 6 to 8 servings

- - - - - - - - - - - -

4 cups halved grape tomatoes

3 cups sprouted wheat berries (see page 30 for sprouting instructions)

2 cups shelled fresh peas, or frozen and thawed

I cup coarsely chopped arugula

$\frac{1}{4}$ cup coarsely chopped fresh cilantro leaves

6 tablespoons freshly squeezed lemon juice

6 tablespoons cold pressed extra virgin olive oil

$\frac{1}{2}$ teaspoon sea salt

$\frac{1}{4}$ teaspoon coarsely ground black pepper

FYI . . .

Cilantro is a member of the carrot family and is also called "coriander" or "Chinese parsley." Additionally, many ancient legends report that cilantro has aphrodisiac qualities.

Pizza With Roasted Red Bell Peppers and Sun-Dried Tomatoes

Yield: 4 to 6 pizzas
(6 inches)

• • • • • • • •

4 sun-dried tomatoes

$1/2$ cup water

2 cloves garlic

I cup ground raw flax
seeds

I cup sprouted wheat
berries (see page 30 for
sprouting instructions)

$1/2$ cup chopped yellow
onion

$1/2$ cup chopped fresh
cilantro

$1/4$ cup chopped fresh basil

I teaspoon sea salt

Topping

2 red bell peppers, sliced

3 tablespoons freshly
squeezed lemon juice

I tablespoon cold pressed
extra virgin olive oil

$1/2$ teaspoon salt

2 cups Marinara Sauce
(page 55)

2 cups Cashew "Cheese"
(page 53)

*This recipe is great for a special occasion, because it will
leave even your non-raw food friends begging for more.
The crust takes a day to dehydrate, so be sure to
prepare this the day before you plan on serving it.*

1. Place the sun-dried tomatoes in the water and soak for 1 hour,
or until soft. Drain the tomatoes and discard the soaking water.

2. To make the crust, place the softened tomatoes and the rest of
the ingredients in a food processor and mix until well-blended.

3. Moisten hands and remove the mixture from the food processor. Using your hands, spread the dough into 4 to 6 flat rounds on
dehydrator sheets.

4. Dehydrate at 105°F for 12 hours. (If you don't own a dehydrator, see page 5 for instructions on how to use an oven for this purpose.) Flip the crusts, then dehydrate for 12 more hours, or until
desired crunchiness is reached. (For directions on how to flip, see
page 6.)

5. While the crust is dehydrating, prepare the topping by putting
the red bell peppers, lemon juice, olive oil, and salt in a medium
bowl. Mix together, then let marinate for at least 4 hours in the
refrigerator.

6. After the crusts have been removed from the dehydrator, layer
the toppings on each one in the following order: Marinara Sauce,
Cashew "Cheese," and marinated red bell peppers. Serve warm.

FOR A CHANGE . . .

● Substitute Pesto (page 56) for Marinara Sauce.

● Add chopped scallions, chopped tomatoes marinated in 1 tablespoon lemon juice and 1 tablespoon olive oil, and/or thinly-sliced mushrooms in addition to—or in place of—the red bell pepper topping.

● Top each pizza with fresh basil, chopped fresh Italian parsley, fresh cilantro, red chili pepper flakes, scallions, chopped fresh rosemary, and/or thyme.

Cashew "Cheese"

This versatile "cheese" can be used in place of traditional cheese in many dishes.

1. Place the cashews in a food processor and chop until completely ground. Keeping the food processor on, gradually add the lemon juice and salt. Once combined, add cool water 1 tablespoon at a time until the substance reaches a cream cheese-like consistency. You may need to stop the food processor several times to scrape down the sides.

2. Use immediately, or transfer to a container and refrigerate until ready to use.

FOR A CHANGE . . .

● Add a few tablespoons of fresh rosemary, cilantro, or your herb of choice.

Yield: About 1 1/2 cups

1 cup raw or untoasted cashews

3 tablespoons freshly squeezed lemon juice

1/4 teaspoon sea salt, or to taste

Basic Italian Marinade

Yield: About 2 cups

- - - - - - - - - -

I bay leaf

$^{1}/_{2}$ cup cold pressed extra virgin olive oil

$^{1}/_{4}$ cup freshly squeezed lemon juice

$^{1}/_{4}$ cup water

$^{1}/_{4}$ cup oil-cured black or kalamata olives

$^{1}/_{4}$ cup coarsely chopped celery

$^{1}/_{8}$ cup coarsely chopped fresh thyme

$^{1}/_{8}$ cup coarsely chopped fresh Italian parsley

$^{1}/_{8}$ cup coarsely chopped fresh oregano

2 tablespoons black peppercorns

I teaspoon sea salt

I teaspoon grated lemon rind

This light, fragrant marinade is a great way to add delicious Italian flavor to any vegetable.

1. Combine all of the ingredients in a medium bowl.

2. Cut your favorite vegetable or vegetables into slices and add to the mixture. Cover, then let marinate for 2 to 3 days in the refrigerator.

3. To serve, remove the vegetables from the marinade and place on a serving platter. Let sit until they reach room temperature, then serve.

TASTES GREAT WITH . . .

Tomatos, red bell peppers, and/or zucchini.

TIP . . .

When grating lemons for lemon rind, only grate the yellow part. Once you reach the white part, the taste is quite bitter.

Marinara Sauce

This is a fantastic tomato sauce that
is easy to prepare but tastes
as if you spent all day making it!

1. Soak the sun-dried tomatoes in the water for 1 hour, or until soft. Reserving the soaking water, drain the tomatoes.

2. Place the tomatoes in a food processor. Add all of the remaining ingredients except the soaking water, and pulse until fully incorporated. Gradually add the reserved tomato water until sauce reaches the desired consistency (you may not use it all).

3. Use immediately, or transfer the sauce to a container and refrigerate until ready to use.

FOR A CHANGE . . .

• Add any of your favorite spices to the sauce, such as oregano or thyme.

Yield: About 5 cups

2 cups sun-dried tomatoes

4 cups cold water

4 cloves garlic

I cup raw or untoasted pine nuts

I cup coarsely chopped fresh basil

I cup coarsely chopped fresh cilantro leaves

$^{1}/_{2}$ cup cold pressed extra virgin olive oil

I teaspoon sea salt

FYI . . .

Pine nuts are a natural source of pinolenic acid, a beneficial hormone stimulant. They are also rich in magnesium, which helps relieve muscle cramps and tension.

Pesto

This sauce is a lighter version of traditional pesto.
It is a great way to incorporate extra greens into your diet.

Yield: About 2¹/₂ cups

¹/₂ cup raw or untoasted walnut halves

I cup chopped fresh basil

¹/₂ cup cold pressed extra virgin olive oil

¹/₂ cup arugula

¹/₄ cup fresh cilantro leaves

3 tablespoons freshly squeezed lemon juice

I teaspoon sea salt

1. Place the walnuts in a food processor and pulse until completely ground. Add the remaining ingredients and mix until well-blended.

2. Use immediately, or transfer the sauce to a container and refrigerate until ready to use. If refrigerating, allow the dressing to return to room temperature and stir vigorously before using.

FOR A CHANGE . . .

● Use spinach or dandelion greens in place of the arugula.

Sun-Dried Tomato Pesto

This pesto is a unique and delicious alternate to basil pesto.
It tastes great as a topping for soups, salads, and raw pastas.

Yield: About I¹/₂ cups

I cup sun-dried tomatoes

2 cups cold water

¹/₂ cup chopped fresh basil

¹/₄ cup cold pressed extra virgin olive oil, plus more to drizzle

¹/₂ teaspoon sea salt

1. Soak the sun-dried tomatoes in the water for 1 hour, or until soft. Drain the tomatoes and discard the water.

2. In a food processor, combine the tomatoes, basil, olive oil, and sea salt. Pulse until smooth. If desired, add more olive oil until the sauce reaches your desired consistency.

3. Use immediately, or transfer the sauce to a container and refrigerate until ready to use.

TASTES GREAT WITH . . .

Zuchini "Fettuccini" (page 50) or Fajitas (page 72).

Strawberries with Balsamic Glaze and Whipped Cream

This simple Italian glaze really compliments the flavors of the strawberries. The flavors stand out more when served at room temperature, so try to prepare just before serving. If necessary, the dish can be refrigerated—just be sure to remove and let stand for one hour at room temperature before serving. For best results, buy organic strawberries and a good quality balsamic vinegar.

Yield: 4 to 6 servings

• • • • • • • •

8 cups strawberries

2 tablespoons raw honey

2 tablespoons balsamic vinegar

Whipped Cream

1 cup raw or untoasted pine nuts

2 tablespoons raw honey

Seeds from $1/2$ vanilla bean, or $1/2$ teaspoon organic vanilla extract

1. Removing the stems, slice the strawberries. Place in a large bowl and mix with the honey. Let marinate for 1 hour at room temperature.

2. To prepare the whipped cream, place the pine nuts in a food processor and pulse until completely ground. Add the honey and vanilla and mix well. If necessary, add water 1 tablespoon at a time to reach the desired cream consistency. You may need to stop the food processor several times to scrape down the sides.

3. Just before serving, toss the strawberries with the balsamic vinegar. Top with whipped cream and serve at room temperature.

FOR A CHANGE . . .

• Try this recipe with any seasonal berry, like blueberries or blackberries.

FYI . . .

Even if you don't buy organic all of the time, strawberries are a fruit that you should buy organic whenever possible. Strawberries have lots of little pockets where pesticides can reside—buying organic strawberries will help you avoid pesticide residue.

Chocolate Cherry Biscotti

*These cookies taste so decadent and exquisite
that you will never miss the baked version.*

Yield: 16 to 20 cookies

· · · · · · · ·

¹/₂ cup dates

1 cup water

1 cup raw or untoasted
almonds

1 cup raw or untoasted
cashews

¹/₂ teaspoon organic vanilla
extract

¹/₈ teaspoon sea salt

1 cup coarsely chopped
raw or untoasted
hazelnuts

1 cup dried unsweetened
cherries

1 cup cacao nibs

1. Place the dates in the water and let soak for 1 hour, or until soft. Reserving the soaking water, drain the dates and set them aside.

2. Place the almonds and cashews in a food processor and chop until finely ground. Add the dates, vanilla, and salt. Mix until well-blended. If necessary, add the reserved soaking water 1 or 2 tablespoons at a time until the mixture has a cookie dough-like consistency.

3. Transfer the mixture to a large bowl and fold in the hazelnuts, cherries, and cacao nibs.

4. With wet hands, divide the dough in half to form 2 long, flat, logs. Cutting at a slight diagonal, divide each log into 8 to 10 biscotti.

5. Eat as is, or transfer the biscotti to dehydrator trays and dehydrate at 105°F for 12 hours. (If you don't own a dehydrator, see page 5 for instructions on how to use an oven for this purpose.) Once dehydrated, serve immediately. To store, place in an airtight container and keep at room temperature, or refrigerate.

FOR A CHANGE . . .

- Substitute raw or untoasted brazil nuts or pistachios for the hazelnuts.

- Use almond extract instead of vanilla extract.

- Use diced dried apricots instead of cherries.

Honey Pine Nut Tart

This is a raw adaptation of a classic Italian dessert. Even without the butter and cream, this tart packs amazing flavor! If possible, use a springform pan with removable sides, since it is difficult to keep that tart's shape when cutting it out of a traditional pie pan.

1. To make the crust, place the almonds in a food processor and pulse until they are a fine powder. Add the honey and mix until smooth.

2. With wet hands, remove the crust from the food processor and mold into the bottom of a 9-inch tart pan that is at least $1\frac{1}{4}$ inches deep. Set aside.

3. To make the filling, pulse the pine nuts in a food processor until they are a fine powder. Add the remaining filling ingredients and mix until smooth. You may need to stop the food processor several times to scrape down the sides.

4. Pour the filling into the crust and spread it out evenly.

5. With wet fingers, press the pine nut topping evenly into the top of the tart.

6. Place the tart in the refrigerator for a few hours before serving (if you are pressed for time, place it in the freezer for 1 hour). Carefully remove the sides of the tart pan and cut the tart. Serve chilled.

FOR A CHANGE . . .

● Make a sweet cream by mixing 2 tablespoons raw honey with 1 cup Cashew "Cheese" (page 53). Add 1 tablespoon to each piece before serving.

Yield: 6 to 8 servings

2 cups raw or untoasted almonds

$\frac{1}{4}$ cup raw honey

Filling

I cup raw or untoasted pine nuts

$\frac{1}{3}$ cup raw honey

I teaspoon lemon rind

$\frac{1}{2}$ teaspoon organic vanilla extract

$\frac{1}{4}$ teaspoon almond extract, preferably organic

Topping

I cup raw or untoasted pine nuts

Dark Chocolate Almond Mousse

This is an amazingly simple, healthy, and decadent dessert. Your friends and family will never guess that the secret ingredient is avocados—what a way to eat your vegetables!

Yield: About 4 servings (roughly $1/3$ cup each)

• • • • • •

2 avocados, preferably Haas

I cup cacao nibs

$1/3$ cup raw cacao powder

$1/4$ cup raw honey

I $1/2$ teaspoons almond extract

$1/8$ teaspoon sea salt

1. Cut each avocado in half and discard the pits. Scoop the meat out of the shells and place it in a food processor.

2. Add the remaining ingredients to the food processor and mix until smooth and creamy.

3. Scoop the mousse onto serving plates and serve.

FOR A CHANGE . . .

● Use hazelnut extract instead of the almond extract for a delicious variation.

● Top each serving with a heaping tablespoon of finely chopped raw almonds or hazelnuts.

3

Mexican Raw Cuisine

The bold flavors of Mexican food lend themselves naturally to raw food cuisine. In this chapter, fresh, authentic ingredients like corn, avocado, tomato, and cilantro have been used to adapt classic Mexican meals to meet raw food standards. From soups and salads to meals and desserts, this chapter will help you find everything you need to make the most beautiful, healthy, and traditional raw Mexican meals. Additionally, the menu ideas on the next page will help you take the guesswork out of meal planning. I have created menus for both a simple and an elegant Mexican meal. For each one, the recipes paired together complement each other beautifully, really bringing out the Mexican essence of each dish.

Menu Ideas

The following menu ideas will transform your kitchen into a healthy, delicious Mexican eatery. I have included sample menus below to help you make either a simple Mexican meal or an elegant Mexican feast. Whether you are pressed for time or have time to spare, the menus are designed so that the flavors of each course complement one another to provide a blissful and authentic Mexican meal.

A Simple and Quick Mexican Meal
(Prepare right before serving)

Mexican Corn, Tomato, and Avocado Salad

Stuffed Peppers

Banana Dream with Cashew Cream

An Elegant Feast
(Requires extra time and equipment)

Corn Chips with Guacamole
(begin the night before to dehydrate the chips)

Fajitas
(make the morning of the day you want
to serve to allow dehydration time)

Chocolate Chili Kisses
(make the night before so they are ready
to serve by dinnertime the following day)

Chilled Avocado Tomato Soup

This creamy soup is a hearty beginning to any meal.

1. To make the topping, place the avocados and cucumber in a medium bowl. Add the cilantro, lemon juice, and sea salt, and mix well. Let marinate for about 5 minutes while you prepare the rest of the soup.

2. Place all the soup ingredients in a food processor. Process until smooth, adding water 1 to 2 tablespoons at a time until the desired consistency is reached.

3. Ladle the soup into bowls, skimming off any foam that may have formed at the top. Scoop a heaping spoonful of topping onto each portion and serve.

FOR A CHANGE . . .

● Add additional toppings, such as diced red bell peppers, diced yellow tomatoes, or diced jicama.

TASTES GREAT WITH . . .

Corn Chips (page 64).

Yield: 4 to 6 servings

2 cloves garlic

1 cucumber, peeled and roughly chopped

4 cups cherry tomatoes

1 cup fresh corn kernels, or frozen and thawed

$1/4$ cup cold pressed extra virgin olive oil

2 tablespoons freshly squeezed lime juice

2 tablespoons freshly squeezed lemon juice

1 teaspoon ground cumin

1 teaspoon sea salt

$1/2$ teaspoon red chili pepper flakes

Topping

2 ripe avocados, cubed

1 cucumber, peeled and cubed

$1/4$ cup chopped fresh cilantro

3 tablespoons freshly squeezed lemon juice

$1/2$ teaspoon sea salt

Corn Chips

I like to triple this recipe and have a huge batch of these on hand—it helps me resist the temptation to indulge on fried corn chips! Plus, these chips take extra time to prepare so you save time by making more at once.

Yield: 6 to 8 servings

- - - - - - - -

2 cloves garlic

2 cups fresh corn kernels, or frozen and thawed

I cup ground flax seed

$^{1}/_{4}$ cup coarsely chopped red onion

2 tablespoons freshly squeezed lime juice

I teaspoon sea salt

I teaspoon white miso

1. Place all of the ingredients in a food processor and mix until smooth.

2. Spread a $^{1}/_{4}$-inch thick layer of the mixture out onto Teflex dehydrator sheets. Dehydrate at 105°F for 12 hours. (If you don't own a dehydrator, see page 5 for instructions on how to use an oven for this purpose.) Flip over and dehydrate for 3 more hours until cohesive, but still soft. (For directions on how to flip, see page 6.)

3. Score the corn sheet into chip-size portions. (If they don't break easily, don't force them.) Dehydrate for an additional 3 hours until the chips are crunchy and break apart easily.

4. Serve immediately, or store in a container at room temperature.

FOR A CHANGE . . .

- In addition to, or instead of, the garlic, use 1 teaspoon red chili pepper flakes, $^{1}/_{2}$ teaspoon cracked black or pink peppercorns, $^{1}/_{2}$ teaspoon dried chipotle pepper, 1 teaspoon chopped fresh oregano, or rosemary.

TASTES GREAT WITH . . .

Black "Bean" Dip (page 65), Guacamole (page 66), or Salsa (page 67).

Black "Bean" Dip

*Using sunflower seeds in place of beans
makes this delicious dip so much easier for our
bodies to digest than the traditional recipe.*

Yield: About 2 cups

- - - - - - - -

I cup sunflower seeds

4 cups warm water

I cup sun-dried tomatoes

2 cloves garlic

$1/_4$ cup cilantro leaves

2 tablespoons cold
pressed extra virgin
olive oil

I teaspoon ground cumin

I teaspoon chili powder

$1/_2$ teaspoon dried Spanish
smoked paprika

$1/_2$ teaspoon dried chipotle
powder

1. Place the sunflower seeds in a small bowl and add 2 cups of the water. Soak overnight or for 12 hours, then drain the seeds and set them aside.

2. Soak the tomatoes in the remaining 2 cups of water for 1 hour at room temperature. Reserving the soaking water, drain the tomatoes.

3. Place the tomatoes and the remaining ingredients (except the soaking water) in a food processor and mix until well-blended. If needed, add the tomato soaking water 1 to 2 tablespoons at a time until the desired consistency is reached.

3. Transfer the dip to a small bowl. Serve immediately, or refrigerate until ready to use. If refrigerating, allow the dip to return to room temperature and stir vigorously before serving.

TASTES GREAT WITH . . .

Carrot sticks or Corn Chips (page 64).

FYI . . .

Sunflower seeds are an exceptionally good source of vitamin E, which reduces inflammation in the body.

Guacamole

No Mexican meal would be complete without guacamole! This recipe is so simple and it allows the flavors of whatever food it accompanies to stand out. For best results, use Haas avocados.

Yield: About 2 cups

. . . .

2 ripe avocados

1 cup quartered grape tomatoes

1/4 cup coarsely chopped fresh cilantro

3 tablespoons freshly squeezed lemon juice

1 teaspoon sea salt

1. Cut each avocado in half and scoop the flesh into a medium bowl. Set the shells aside.

2. Place all of the remaining ingredients in the bowl and combine with a fork until just mixed, but still chunky.

3. Serve immediately, or transfer to a container and refrigerate until ready to use.

TASTES GREAT WITH . . .

Corn Chips (page 64), your favorite vegetable, or Mexican Slaw (page 69).

FOR A CHANGE . . .

● Use the avocado shells as bowls. Scoop the guacamole into the avocado shells and serve.

TIP . . .

Because avocados are particularly sensitive to browning when exposed to oxygen, it is best to prepare the guacamole right before serving.

Salsa

*This salsa tastes so fresh, you will never want
to go back to the store-bought variety.*

1. Remove the seeds and white membranes from inside the
chile. Dice the chile, and place it in a large bowl. Add the
remaining ingredients and combine.

2. Let the salsa marinate for at least 20 minutes at room
temperature. Serve immediately, or transfer the salsa to a
container and refrigerate until ready to use.

FOR A CHANGE . . .

• Use yellow and/or orange teardrop tomatoes instead of
the cherry tomatoes.

TASTES GREAT WITH . . .

Corn Chips (page 64).

Yield: About 4 cups

. . . .

$1/2$ poblano chile

2 shallots, finely diced

2 cups quartered cherry
tomatoes

I cup finely diced scallions

$1/2$ cup finely chopped fresh
cilantro leaves

$1/4$ cup finely chopped fresh
Italian parsley

$1/4$ cup cold pressed extra virgin
olive oil

3 tablespoons freshly squeezed
lemon juice

2 teaspoons freshly squeezed
lime juice

I teaspoon sea salt

Mexican Corn, Tomato, and Avocado Salad

Yield: 4 to 6 servings

2 ripe avocados, cut into 1-inch cubes

2 cups fresh corn kernels, or frozen and thawed

2 cups quartered grape tomatoes

1 cup coarsely chopped fresh cilantro leaves

$^1/_2$ cup chopped scallions

$^1/_3$ cup Mexican Lemon Cumin Dressing (page 69)

Topping

$^1/_4$ cup diced orange peppers

$^1/_4$ cup diced red bell peppers

This salad is a favorite in my house. It is particularly delicious if you use fresh corn from the cob and Haas avocados.

1. Combine the avocados, corn, tomatoes, cilantro, and scallions in a large bowl. Add the dressing and gently toss.

2. Top the salad with the orange and red bell peppers for a visual treat. Serve immediately.

FOR A CHANGE . . .

● Add $^1/_4$ cup diced yellow tomatoes to the top of the salad as well to make the meal even more visually appealing.

TASTES GREAT WITH . . .

Tacos (page 71) or Fajitas (page 72).

Mexican Slaw

This is an exciting twist on traditional coleslaw. It makes a great side dish, and even works as a topping for raw fajitas.

1. Combine the carrots, beet, and jicama in a large bowl. Add the dressing and mix well. Let marinate for 1 hour at room temperature.

2. Serve as is, or top the slaw with Guacamole (page 66) and Salsa (page 67) for a flavorful, hearty lunch.

Yield: 4 to 6 servings

2 medium carrots, shredded

1 cup shredded beet

1 cup shredded jicama

$^1/_2$ cup Cilantro Chili Dressing (page 70)

FOR A CHANGE . . .

● Substitute any of the following vegetables for a different, but still delicious, taste: 1 cup shredded, peeled broccoli stems in place of the beet, 1 cup shredded parsnips in place of the jicama, or 1 cup shredded zucchini in place of the carrots.

Mexican Lemon Cumin Dressing

This dressing combines the fresh flavor of lemon with the bold and smoky flavors of cumin and chipotle pepper. It is so light and flavorful that it just may become a household favorite.

1. Place all the ingredients in a jar with a lid (a Mason jar is good). Cover and shake well until all of the ingredients are combined.

2. Use the dressing immediately, or refrigerate until ready to use. If refrigerating, allow the dressing to return to room temperature and stir vigorously before serving.

Yield: About 1 cup

$^1/_2$ cup cold pressed extra virgin olive oil

$^1/_2$ cup freshly squeezed lemon juice

1 teaspoon ground cumin

1 teaspoon sea salt

1 teaspoon chili powder

$^1/_2$ teaspoon chipotle pepper powder

cilantro chili Dressing

The classic flavors of cilantro, lime, and
cumin are combined in this exciting dressing.
Add it to any salad for a Mexican twist.

Yield: About 1 cup

3 cloves garlic, finely chopped

$^1/_2$ cup cold pressed extra
virgin olive oil

$^1/_2$ cup finely chopped
cilantro leaves

4 tablespoons freshly
squeezed lemon juice

4 tablespoons freshly
squeezed lime juice

1 $^1/_2$ teaspoons ground cumin

1 teaspoon red chili
pepper flakes

1. Place all the ingredients in a jar with a lid (a Mason jar is good). Cover and shake well until all of the ingredients are combined.

2. Use the dressing immediately, or refrigerate until ready to use. If refrigerating, allow the dressing to return to room temperature and stir vigorously before serving.

Tomato chili Dressing

This thick, creamy dressing combines the classic flavors of tomato and chili, creating a hearty topping for any salad.

Yield: About 2 cups

$^1/_2$ cup sun-dried tomatoes

1 cup water

$^1/_2$ cup extra virgin olive oil

$^1/_4$ cup chopped fresh basil

$^1/_4$ cup balsamic vinegar

1 teaspoon ground cumin

$^1/_4$ teaspoon chili powder

$^1/_4$ teaspoon sea salt

1. Place the tomatoes in the water and soak for about 1 hour, or until soft. Transfer the tomatoes and the water to a food processor. Add the remaining ingredients and pulse until the entire mixture is smooth and creamy. More water can be added 1 to 2 tablespoons at a time if the final consistency is too thick.

2. Use the dressing immediately, or refrigerate until ready to use. If refrigerating, allow the dressing to return to room temperature and stir vigorously before serving.

Tacos

This raw version of the famous Mexican dish uses romaine lettuce leaves in place of taco shells. These tacos look so beautiful on a platter, and they are great for parties. They take a little extra time to prepare, since the walnuts need to soak overnight. However, be sure to finish preparations just before serving, as the lettuce will wilt.

Yield: 6 to 8 servings

I cup raw or untoasted walnuts

2 cups water

I tablespoon nutritional yeast

I teaspoon Bragg Liquid Aminos or tamari soy sauce

I cup Black "Bean" Dip (page 65)

I cup Guacamole (page 66)

I cup Salsa (page 67)

16 large romaine lettuce leaves

1. Place the walnuts in the water and allow them to soak overnight, or about 12 hours. Drain, then place the walnuts in a food processor.

2. Pulse the walnuts until they look like large crumbs. Add the nutritional yeast and the Bragg and pulse until all of the ingredients are combined. Be sure to stop pulsing before the mixture becomes mushy—the final consistency should still have some texture.

3. To assemble the tacos, first place a layer of the walnut "meat" on each romaine shell. Next, add a layer of Black "Bean" Dip, then a layer of Guacamole, and finally a layer of Salsa. Arrange the tacos on a plate and serve immediately.

FOR A CHANGE . . .

● Add a spoonful of Cashew "Cheese" (page 53) or Molé Sauce (page 73) to the top of each taco for a more intense flavor.

Fajitas

These hearty fajitas are bursting with delicious, natural flavor, and they are a great way to stay raw when you really feel the need to indulge. Allow extra time to prepare this meal, because the sunflower seeds need to soak overnight. Additionally, you should start making the tortillas first thing in the morning if you want them ready for dinner.

Yield: 4 to 6 servings

1 cup sunflower seeds

2 cups water

$1/2$ medium red bell pepper, chopped

2 cups frozen corn kernels

$1/4$ cup chopped yellow onion

1 teaspoon ground cumin

1 teaspoon raw honey

$1/2$ teaspoon chili flakes

Filling

1 red bell pepper, thinly sliced

1 clove garlic, chopped

$1/2$ cup thinly sliced red onion

3 tablespoons freshly squeezed lemon juice

3 tablespoons cold pressed extra virgin olive oil

1 teaspoon sea salt

$1/2$ teaspoon ground cumin

$1/2$ teaspoon red chili pepper flakes

1. Place the seeds in the water and allow them to soak overnight, or about 12 hours. Drain and rinse the seeds, then drain again.

2. To make the tortillas, place the sunflower seeds in a food processor. Add the remaining ingredients and combine until smooth.

3. Transfer the tortilla mixture to Teflex dehydrator sheets, making 4-inch round circles that are $1/4$-inch thick. (You should be able to make 4 to 6 circles.) Dehydrate at 105°F for 4 hours. (If you don't own a dehydrator, see page 5 for instructions on how to use an oven for this purpose.)

4. After 4 hours, carefully flip the tortillas over and dehydrate for another 4 to 6 hours. (For directions on how to flip, see page 6.) When the tortillas are finished "cooking," they will appear dry but will still be flexible.

5. After you flip the tortillas, prepare the fajita filling. Combine all of the filling ingredients in a medium bowl, mix, then let marinate in the refrigerator for 4 hours.

6. Remove the vegetables from the refrigerator and let sit at room temperature for at least 30 minutes. Remove the tortillas from the dehydrator and fill with the marinated vegetables. Serve immediately.

FOR A CHANGE . . .

● Marinate different types of vegetables to add to or replace the filling, such as: shredded zucchini, shredded carrots, corn, diced tomatoes, finely diced eggplant, diced garlic, and/or chopped olives.

● Top each fajita with Guacamole (page 66) or Mole Sauce (below) for a more intense flavor.

● Add $1/2$ teaspoon smoked Spanish paprika to the filling ingredients.

Molé Sauce

I have adapted this classic Mexican sauce to meet raw food standards. It is bursting with flavor and authenticity.

1. Place the tomatoes in the water and soak for 1 hour, or until soft. Reserving the soaking water, remove the tomatoes.

2. Place the tomatoes and all of the remaining ingredients (except the soaking water) in a food processor. Combine until smooth. Add the reserved tomato water 1 tablespoon at a time until the desired consistency is reached.

3. Use immediately, or transfer to a container and refrigerate until ready to use.

TASTES GREAT WITH . . .

Tacos (page 71), Fajitas (page 72), or Stuffed Peppers (page 74).

Yield: About 2 cups

1 cup sun-dried tomatoes

2 cups warm water

2 cloves garlic

$1/4$ cup finely ground raw or untoasted pistachios

$1/4$ cup chopped red onion

2 tablespoons raw almond butter

1 tablespoon chili powder

$1/2$ teaspoon ground coriander

$1/2$ teaspoon cinnamon

$1/2$ teaspoon sea salt

$1/4$ teaspoon cloves

Stuffed Peppers

*These peppers are delicious no matter what,
but are particularly satisfying if you dehydrate
them for four hours before serving.*

Yield: 6 servings

I cup sun-dried tomatoes

2 cups warm water

I cup raw or untoasted
walnuts

I clove garlic

$1/2$ cup chopped fresh
Italian parsley

$1/4$ cup chopped red onion

I teaspoon ground
chipotle pepper

$1/2$ teaspoon sea salt

I medium zucchini, peeled
and shredded

$1/8$ cup cold pressed extra
virgin olive oil

3 large red bell peppers,
halved and scooped out

1. Place the tomatoes in the water and soak for about 1 hour, or until soft. Reserving the soaking liquid, remove the tomatoes and set aside.

2. Place the walnuts in a food processor and chop until they are a fine powder. Add the soaked tomatoes, garlic, parsley, onion, chipotle pepper, and salt. Continue mixing until all of the ingredients are chopped and mixed well into a paste-like consistency.

3. Transfer the mixture to a large bowl. Add the zucchini, olive oil, and $1/8$ cup of the reserved tomato water. Mix by hand until the substance is moist, but not runny.

4. Scoop this filling evenly into the red bell pepper halves. Serve immediately, or dehydrate at 105°F for 4 to 6 hours.

FOR A CHANGE . . .

● For a more intense flavor, top each pepper with 1 tablespoon Guacamole (page 66) and 1 tablespoon Salsa (page 67), or with 1 tablespoon Molé Sauce (page 73).

● Use an assortment of sweet colored bell peppers, such as green, red, orange, yellow, and purple, rather than just red.

Chocolate Chili Kisses

These cookies are a fantastic end to any feast, as they combine the classic Mexican flavors of cocoa and chili.

1. Place the dates in the water and soak for 1 hour, or until soft. Discarding the water, remove the dates and set them aside.

2. Put the pecans in a food processor and chop until they are a fine powder. Add the dates, and continue to process until the mixture is well-blended.

3. Add all of the remaining ingredients to the food processor and pulse until well-blended.

4. Drop the dough by rounded teaspoons onto Teflex sheets. Dehydrate at 105°F for 24 hours. Remove from the dehydrator and serve.

FOR A CHANGE . . .

● Drop the dough onto cookie trays and freeze for 1 hour instead of dehydrating.

Yield: 20 to 24 cookies

1 cup dates

2 cups water

1 cup raw or untoasted pecans

$1/4$ cup raw honey

$1/2$ cup cacao powder, or organic pure cocoa powder

1 teaspoon organic vanilla extract

$1/2$ teaspoon salt

$1/2$ teaspoon chili powder

$1/8$ teaspoon cayenne powder

TIP . . .

If freezing, keeping the cookies in the freezer for 1 hour will ensure a firm consistency. However, the cookies can be stored for longer than 1 hour in the freezer. If you do this, allow the cookies to soften a bit in the refrigerator or at room temperature before serving.

Banana Dream with Orange Cashew Cream

Yield: 4 servings

. . . .

4 ripe bananas

3 tablespoons raw honey

$^1/_2$ teaspoon cinnamon

Orange Cashew Cream

1 cup raw or untoasted cashews

$^1/_4$ cup freshly squeezed orange juice

3 tablespoons raw honey

This is a raw adaptation of fried bananas, a classic Mexican dessert. This version is so delicious and so good for you, you could eat it for breakfast!

1. Remove the skins from the bananas and place each banana on a serving plate. Cut the bananas on a slight diagonal into 1-inch slices.

2. Drizzle the honey over the bananas, then top each banana with a dusting of cinnamon. Set the bananas aside.

3. To make the cream, place the cashews in a food processor and pulse until they are a fine powder. Add the orange juice and honey nectar and continue to pulse until well-blended.

4. Place a dollop of cream on each banana and serve.

FOR A CHANGE . . .

● In addition to, or instead of, bananas, use 2 mangos cut into $^1/_2$-inch cubes; 2 very ripe pears cut into $^1/_2$-inch wedges; or 1 cup fresh seasonal berries.

4

Middle Eastern Raw Cuisine

After spending several years living and eating in the Middle East, writing this chapter was a welcome challenge. I was so excited to take the bold flavors of the region I had grown to love and form them into healthy and delicious raw meals. Finally finishing this chapter was so rewarding. Quite frankly, I think the raw versions of hummus and falafel you will find in this chapter are even more delicious than the versions you will find at any of the roadside stands scattered throughout the Middle East.

If you are planning a Middle Eastern meal, be sure to check out the Menu Ideas section on the next page. Whether you are looking to make a simple meal or an elegant feast, I've included ideas to help you turn your kitchen into a Middle Eastern eatery.

Menu Ideas

The following menus will provide you with ideas for how to create and enjoy the finest Middle Eastern regional flavors with ease and grace. The quick meal, which consists of of hummus, dolmas, and figs, is a fresh and light version of a classic meal with flavors that complement each other well. If, however, you have the time to set aside for the elegant feast, I recommend doing so. You can impress your family and friends while taking the guesswork out of timing the more complicated—but equally mouthwatering—raw food delicacies.

A Simple and Quick Middle Eastern Meal
(Prepare right before serving)

Hummus
(served with carrots and celery sticks)

Dolmas with Lemon Tahini Dressing

Fresh Figs Drizzled in Honey and Cacao

An Elegant Feast
(Requires extra time and equipment)

Breadsticks with Za'atar Dipping Sauce
(begin the night before to dehydrate)

Sprouted Chickpea Falafel with classic Middle Eastern Salad and Lemon Tahini Dressing
(begin sprouting the chickpeas three days before the meal;
prepare and dehydrate the falafel the morning of the feast)

Baklava (make one hour before your guests arrive
and refrigerate until ready to serve)

Hummus

This classic Middle Eastern appetizer is a great introduction to raw foods. You will be amazed at how easy this is to prepare, and how much lighter it tastes than traditional hummus. For best results, use a high quality, cold pressed olive oil.

1. Place all of the ingredients in a food processor and mix until smooth and creamy. You may have to shut the food processor off several times to scrape the sides.

2. Transfer the hummus to a medium bowl. For the topping, drizzle the olive oil over the hummus, then sprinkle the paprika as a finishing touch. Serve immediately, or refrigerate until ready to use.

FOR A CHANGE . . .

• Add one of the following ingredients to the hummus before mixing for an unusual but tasty twist: $\frac{1}{2}$ cup chopped kalamata olives, $\frac{1}{2}$ cup chopped red bell pepper, 2 tablespoons chopped fresh rosemary, 1 tablespoon chipotle chili powder, or $\frac{1}{4}$ teaspoon cardamom.

TASTES GREAT WITH . . .

Carrot sticks, celery sticks, Tabouleh (page 86), or Sprouted Chickpea Falafel (page 88).

Yield: About 3 cups

3 cloves garlic, coarsely chopped

2 medium zucchini, peeled and coarsely chopped (about 1 $\frac{1}{2}$ cups)

1 medium carrot, peeled and coarsely chopped

1 cup raw tahini

$\frac{3}{4}$ cup freshly squeezed lemon juice

$\frac{1}{4}$ cup cold pressed extra virgin olive oil

1 teaspoon sea salt

1 teaspoon ground cumin

Topping

2 tablespoons cold pressed extra virgin olive oil

$\frac{1}{2}$ teaspoon dried paprika

Baba Ganoush

The smoked Spanish paprika is what gives this dip its earthy taste. Plus, it is a healthier alternative to the burnt eggplant used in the traditional Middle Eastern dip.

Yield: About 2 cups

$1/2$ medium eggplant, peeled and cubed (about 1 cup)

$1/2$ cup cold pressed extra virgin olive oil

6 tablespoons freshly squeezed lemon juice

$1 1/2$ teaspoons sea salt

$1/2$ cup raw or untoasted walnut halves

1 clove garlic

1 cup raw tahini

$1/2$ teaspoon ground cumin

$1/2$ teaspoon smoked Spanish paprika

1. Place the eggplant, $1/4$ cup of the olive oil, 3 tablespoons of the lemon juice, and $1/2$ teaspoon of the salt in a medium bowl. Mix, then let marinate for 4 hours in the refrigerator.

2. Place the walnuts in a food processor and pulse until they are a fine powder. Add the marinated eggplant, garlic, tahini, cumin, paprika, and remaining lemon juice, olive oil, and salt. Blend until smooth.

3. Transfer the baba ganoush to a bowl and serve.

TASTES GREAT WITH . . .

Carrot sticks or slices of red bell pepper.

FOR A CHANGE . . .

● Drizzle olive oil and sprinkle smoked Spanish paprika over the dip before serving.

Skordalia

This classic Greek garlic dip is a fantastic addition to any party.

1. Place the almonds in a food processor and blend until they are a fine powder. Add the garlic, jicama, cauliflower, zucchini, and salt and continue blending until smooth.

2. Add the lemon juice and pulse to incorporate.

3. With the food processor running slowly, stream in $1/2$ cup of the olive oil. Continue processing until the dip has a creamy consistency. You may need to stop the food processor several times to scrape down the sides.

4. Transfer the skordalia to a medium bowl. Drizzle the remaining olive oil over the top and serve.

TASTES GREAT WITH . . .

Carrot sticks or Breadsticks (page 82).

FOR A CHANGE . . .

● Sprinkle $1/4$ cup chopped chives over the skordalia.

● Using a mandolin slicer, slice a beet into thin rounds and arrange around the outside of the bowl.

Yield: About $2 1/2$ cups

. . . .

1 cup raw or untoasted almonds

6 cloves garlic

$1/2$ cup peeled, cubed jicama

$1/4$ cup chopped cauliflower

$1/4$ cup peeled, chopped zucchini

1 teaspoon sea salt

1 tablespoon freshly squeezed lemon juice

$3/4$ cup cold pressed extra virgin olive oil

Breadsticks with Za'atar Dipping Sauce

Za'atar is a classic spice mixture found throughout the Middle East. Paired with these breadsticks, this appetizer is similar to typical street food found in many Middle Eastern outdoor markets.

Yield: 15 to 20 breadsticks

. . . .

2 cups raw or untoasted sunflower seeds

1 cup ground flax seed

2 tablespoons freshly squeezed lemon juice

2 tablespoons nutritional yeast

2 teaspoons sea salt

$1/4$ cup of water

4 tablespoons dried oregano

2 tablespoons raw or untoasted sesame seeds

Dipping Sauce

2 tablespoons za'atar (page 83)

1 cup cold pressed extra virgin olive oil

1. Place the sunflower seeds in a food processor and chop until they are a fine powder. Add the flax seed, lemon juice, nutritional yeast, and 1 teaspoon of the sea salt and pulse until the mixture is thoroughly combined.

2. Add the water 1 tablespoon at a time until the dough is cohesive. (You may not need to use all the water.) Leave the dough in the food processor and set aside.

3. On a medium plate, mix the oregano, sesame seeds, and the remaining teaspoon of sea salt.

4. With wet hands, remove the dough from the food processor in golf ball-sized increments. Roll each ball of dough into a breadstick shape, then roll each breadstick through the oregano mixture. Place the breadsticks on a dehydrator sheet and dehydrate at 105°F for 12 to 20 hours, or until the desired crunchiness is reached. (If you don't own a dehydrator, see page 5 for instructions on how to use an oven for this purpose.)

5. While the breadsticks are dehydrating, prepare the dipping sauce by mixing the za'atar and the olive oil in a medium bowl.

6. Remove the breadsticks from the dehydrator and arrange on a serving platter. Place the bowl with the dipping sauce in the middle. Serve and enjoy.

FOR A CHANGE . . .

● Coat the breadsticks with 4 tablespoons raw or untoasted caraway seeds or 4 tablespoons cracked black and pink peppercorns in addition to, or instead of, the oregano mixture.

Za'atar

Za'atar is a spice mixture so common throughout the Middle East that each region has its own version.

Yield: About $1/4$ cup

2 tablespoons dried marjoram

2 tablespoons dried oregano

2 tablespoons dried thyme

1 tablespoon raw or untoasted sesame seeds

1 teaspoon dried coriander

1 teaspoon sea salt

$1/4$ teaspoon dried fennel

1. Place all of the ingredients in a small bowl and combine.

2. Sprinkle the za'atar over your favorite salad and enjoy!

FOR A CHANGE . . .

● Combine 1 tablespoon of za'atar with $1/2$ cup cold pressed extra virgin olive oil to make a delicious dip that tastes great with Breadsticks (page 82).

● Combine 1 tablespoon of za'atar with $1/4$ cup lemon juice and $1/4$ cup cold pressed extra virgin olive oil to make a dressing that pairs well with any salad or vegetable.

Classic Middle Eastern Lemon Dressing

Using a good quality olive oil will really make this dressing taste superb. For best results, use a whisk to mix the ingredients.

Yield: About 1 cup

$1/2$ cup freshly squeezed lemon juice

$1/2$ cup cold pressed extra virgin olive oil

1 teaspoon sea salt

1. Place all of the ingredients in a medium bowl and mix until completely incorporated.

2. Use the dressing immediately, or transfer to a container and refrigerate until ready to use. If refrigerating, allow the dressing to return to room temperature and stir vigorously before using.

TASTES GREAT WITH . . .

Classic Middle Eastern Salad (page 84) and Wilted Spinach Salad (page 85).

Classic Middle Eastern Salad

This Middle Eastern salad is my version of the standard that is found at almost every falafel stand. It makes for a fantastic side dish or a quick lunch.

Yield: 4 to 6 servings

4 large tomatoes, peeled and cubed

3 scallions, chopped

2 cucumbers, peeled and cut into $1/2$-inch cubes

$1/2$ cup Classic Middle Eastern Lemon Dressing (page 83)

1. Place all of the ingredients in a medium bowl and toss. Let stand for 10 minutes at room temperature.

2. Transfer salad to bowls and serve.

FOR A CHANGE . . .

● Soak 1 cup sun-dried tomatoes in 2 cups water for 1 hour, or until soft. Drain the tomatoes, then mix them with the salad and add 1 cup sprouted chickpeas for a heavier meal.

FYI . . .

In some parts of the Middle East this salad is served for breakfast. Now that's a healthy start to the day!

Wilted Spinach Salad with Marinated Eggplant Tapenade

Wilting the spinach, as opposed to cooking it, preserves its vital enzymes and enhances this salad's fresh flavor.

1. To make the tapenade, combine the eggplant, garlic, 1 tablespoon of the olive oil, 1 tablespoon of the lemon juice, and ½ teaspoon of the salt in a medium bowl. Let marinate for 4 hours in the refrigerator.

2. Remove the marinated eggplant from the refrigerator and let sit at room temperature. In a separate bowl, place the tomatoes in the water and soak for 1 hour, or until soft. Reserving the soaking water, remove the tomatoes.

3. In a food processor, combine the tomatoes, marinated eggplant, olives, walnuts, vinegar, and remaining lemon juice, salt, and olive oil. Coarsely chop the ingredients until they become a thick salsa. If necessary, add the reserved tomato water 1 tablespoon at a time until the desired consistency is reached.

4. To make the salad, remove the stems from the spinach and coarsely chop the leaves. Place the spinach and the dressing in a large bowl and toss. Set aside for 5 minutes to allow the spinach to wilt.

5. Transfer the spinach to salad plates. Top each serving with chickpeas and a heaping spoonful of tapenade and serve.

FOR A CHANGE . . .

● Pair the salad with Breadsticks (page 82) for a complete meal.

Yield: 4 to 6 servings

● ● ● ● ● ● ● ● ● ● ●

4 cups baby spinach

½ cup Classic Middle Eastern Lemon Dressing (page 83)

2 cups sprouted chickpeas (see page 30 for sprouting instructions)

Tapenade

½ eggplant, cubed (about ¼ cup)

2 cloves garlic, chopped

3 tablespoons cold pressed extra virgin olive oil

2 tablespoons freshly squeezed lemon juice

1 teaspoon sea salt

1 cup sun-dried tomatoes

2 cups water

¼ cup kalamata olives

1 cup raw or untoasted walnut halves

1 tablespoon balsamic vinegar

Tabouleh

Yield: 4 to 6 servings

· · · · · · · · · · ·

1 cauliflower head, separated
into large florets

4 large tomatoes, diced
(about 2 cups)

4 scallions, chopped

2 cloves garlic, minced

1 large cucumber, peeled
and diced

2 cups sprouted wheat berries
(see page 30 for sprouting
instructions)

1 cup chopped fresh Italian
parsley, stems removed

1 cup Classic Middle Eastern
Lemon Dressing (page 83)

*By using cauliflower and sprouted wheat, you can
enjoy this Middle Eastern delight and feed your body
optimal amounts of enzymes at the same time.*

1. Place the cauliflower in a food processor and pulse until
it resembles fine breadcrumbs.

2. Transfer the cauliflower to a large bowl. Add the
remaining ingredients and mix well. Let marinate for 20
minutes at room temperature.

3. Once marinated, transfer the tabouleh to plates and
serve.

FOR A CHANGE . . .

- Add 1 cup chopped kalamata olives before marinating.
- Season with salt and pepper before serving.

FYI . . .

Ounce per ounce, parsley contains three
times as much vitamin C as oranges!

Creamy Oregano Mint Dressing

*Pine nuts, lemon, fresh oregano, and mint
combine to make this delicious dressing.*

Yield: About 2 cups

1. Place the pine nuts in a food processor and blend until completely chopped. Add the remaining ingredients and pulse until completely incorporated. If necessary, add water 1 teaspoon at a time to reach the desired consistency.

2. Use dressing immediately, or refrigerate until ready to use. If refrigerating, allow the dressing to return to room temperature and stir vigorously before using.

TASTES GREAT WITH . . .

Rustic Tomato Salad (page 44), Classic Middle Eastern Salad (page 84), or Tabouleh (page 86).

1 cup raw or untoasted
pine nuts

1/2 cup freshly squeezed
lemon juice

1/2 cup cold pressed extra
virgin olive oil

2 tablespoons chopped
fresh oregano

2 tablespoons chopped
fresh mint

1 teaspoon sea salt

Lemon Tahini Dressing

*This dressing is a great addition to any Middle Eastern meal.
Serve with falafel, grape leaves, or over any salad
to really bring out its flavor.*

Yield: About 1 1/2 cups

1. In a food processor, combine all of the ingredients except the water. Once combined, add the water 1 to 2 tablespoons at a time until the desired consistency is reached. (You may not need to use all the water.)

2. Use immediately, or transfer the dressing to a container and refrigerate until ready to use.

TASTES GREAT WITH . . .

Tabouleh (page 86), Sprouted Chickpea Falafel (page 88), or Dolmas (page 89).

2 cloves garlic, finely chopped

1 cup raw tahini

4 tablespoons freshly
squeezed lemon juice

1/2 teaspoon sea salt

1/4 cup water

Sprouted Chickpea Falafel

This sprouted chickpea falafel is a lighter version of the fried balls found in authentic Middle Eastern cuisine. The flavor is so fabulously smokey and fresh, you may never want to eat the fried version again!

Yield: 6 to 8 servings

2 cups raw or untoasted almonds

2 cloves garlic

$^1/_2$ red onion, chopped

I cup sprouted chickpeas
(see page 30 for sprouting
instructions)

$^1/_4$ cup raw or untoasted
sesame oil

2 tablespoons Nama shoyu or
tamari soy sauce

I teaspoon ground cumin

I teaspoon chili powder

$^1/_2$ teaspoon dried smoked
Spanish paprika

1. Place the almonds in a food processor and chop until they are a fine powder. Add all of the remaining ingredients and chop until well-blended to create a doughy consistency.

2. With wet hands, form the dough into balls $^1/_2$-inch in diameter. Place the balls on dehydrator screens and dehydrate at 105°F for 4 hours. If the dough seems a bit runny, use a Teflex sheet on top of the screens. (If you don't own a dehydrator, see page 5 for instructions on how to use an oven for this purpose.)

3. Roll each ball over and dehydrate for an additional 4 hours, or until the falafel reach the desired crunchiness.

4. Arrange the falafel on a platter and serve.

FOR A CHANGE . . .

● Serve with 1 cup Salsa (page 67), 1 cup Lemon Tahini Dressing (page 87), or 1 cup Mango Salsa (page 113) for a variety of tastes.

FYI . . .

In many Middle Eastern countries, falafel is served as a streetside fast food, very similar to the way hot dogs are in North America.

Dolmas

*The authentic flavors of mint, lemon,
and pine nut combine to make this meal
a delicious staple for a raw food diet.*

1. Place the cauliflower in a food processor and mix until it resembles fine breadcrumbs. Add the mint, arugula, and parsley and pulse until well-chopped.

2. Transfer the mixture to a large bowl. Add the dressing and stir until well-combined. Stir in the pine nuts and raisins.

3. Arrange the collard leaves on a serving platter. Spoon the cauliflower mixture evenly into the collard leaves. Roll the leaves like burritos and serve.

FOR A CHANGE . . .

● Top each dolma with $\frac{1}{2}$ teaspoon Za'atar (page 83) and 1 teaspoon Lemon Tahini Dressing (page 87).

Yield: 8 to 10 dolmas

1 cup cauliflower florets

$\frac{1}{2}$ cup chopped fresh mint

$\frac{1}{4}$ cup arugula

$\frac{1}{4}$ cup chopped fresh Italian parsley

$\frac{1}{2}$ cup Classic Middle Eastern Lemon Dressing (page 83)

1 cup raw or untoasted pine nuts

$\frac{1}{2}$ cup raisins

8 to 10 collard leaves, bottom stems removed

FYI . . .

For centuries, mint has been used by alternative health practitioners to aid digestion and relieve upset stomachs.

Halvah Truffles

Halvah is a staple dessert in Middle Eastern countries. This raw version, which includes a delicious cacao twist, is extremely easy to prepare!

Yield: 18 to 20 truffles

$^1/_2$ cup dates

I cup water

$^1/_2$ cup raw or untoasted hazelnuts

$^1/_2$ cup raw tahini

$^1/_2$ teaspoon sea salt

$^1/_2$ cup raw cacao nibs

1. Place the dates in the water and let soak for 1 hour, or until soft. Reserving the soaking water, drain the dates and set them aside.

2. Place the hazelnuts in a food processor and pulse until they resemble crumbs. Add the dates, tahini, and salt. Pulse until all the ingredients are combined into a doughy consistency.

3. Spread the cacao nibs out across a medium plate. With wet hands, roll the dough into $^1/_2$-inch balls, then roll each ball through the cacao until well-coated.

4. Place the covered balls on a large plate. Let sit in the freezer for 1 hour. Remove and serve, or place in the refrigerator until ready to serve.

FOR A CHANGE . . .

● Instead of cacao nibs, roll the truffles in $^1/_2$ cup sesame seeds or $^1/_2$ cup raisins mixed with 2 tablespoons cinnamon.

● Place the truffles in a dehydrator for about 4 hours and serve warm.

Baklava

*This raw version of the popular Middle Eastern pastry
is incredibly sweet and satisfying. The tastes of
these pure ingredients really shine, and this dessert
is sure to impress on any special occasion.
I recommend using a mandolin slicer to cut the fruit,
but if you don't have one, a knife will do the trick.*

Yield: 4 to 5 servings

$\frac{1}{2}$ cup raw or untoasted
pistachios

$\frac{1}{2}$ cup raw or untoasted walnuts

3 tablespoons raw honey

2 Asian pears or Granny
Smith apples

1. Place the pistachios and the walnuts in a food processor and pulse until they are completely mixed. Add 2 tablespoons of the honey and mix until fully incorporated.

2. Using a mandolin slicer or knife, cut the pears into 16 to 20 very thin disks.

3. To assemble, place one slice of pear on a plate and top it with a spoonful of the pistachio mixture. Spread the mixture evenly, then place another slice of pear on top. Continue alternating layers until 4 slices of pear have been used.

4. Drizzle the remaining tablespoon of honey over the assembled baklava and serve.

FOR A CHANGE . . .

• Use raw or untoasted hazelnuts in place of the walnuts.

Fresh Figs Drizzled in Honey and Cacao

The irresistible combination of fresh figs and chocolate makes this simple dish unforgettable!

Yield: 6 to 8 servings

12 fresh figs

$^1/_2$ cup raw honey

$^1/_4$ cup cacao powder

1. Cut the figs in half and arrange them on a serving platter with the insides faced up.

2. In a small bowl, combine the honey and cacao and mix well to make a syrup. Drizzle the syrup over the figs and serve.

FOR A CHANGE . . .

● Arrange $^1/_2$ cup fresh seasonal berries around the figs for a visually appealing finish.

FYI . . .

Not only are figs high in fiber, they are a good source of potassium, a mineral linked to controlling blood pressure.

5

Asian Raw Cuisine

The bright, fresh flavors of Asian cuisine shine in this chapter, which focuses on delicacies from the region. Because many Asian recipes already feature an array of fresh, crisp vegetables, you will easily be able to enjoy many of your favorite dishes prepared in a raw food manner without having to make many changes. For this chapter, I have chosen my favorite meals from Japanese, Thai, and Chinese cuisine and adapted them to meet raw food standards.

Don't forget to take a look at the Menu Ideas on the next page for ideas on serving both a simple Asian meal and an elegant Asian feast!

Menu Ideas

The sample menus on this page will allow you to create delicious Asian-inspired meals, whether you are pressed for time or have plenty of time to spare. For both menus, the flavors present in the chosen dishes complement each other beautifully, awakening the senses and allowing you and your guests to fully enjoy Asian cuisine. Preparation time approximations have been given for the elegant feast, so you can prepare it with ease without feeling rushed.

A Simple and Quick Asian Meal
(Prepare right before serving)

Miso Soup

Pad Thai

Pineapple with Ginger Chocolate Fondue

An Elegant Feast
(Requires extra time and equipment)

Cilantro Lime Soup
(begin 1 hour before)

Seaweed Salad with Daikon Dumplings
(begin 1 hour before to marinate the seaweed)

Almond Cookies
(make a day or two before to dehydrate)

MiSo Soup

Miso is a paste that is traditionally made from fermented soybeans. Look for it in the refrigerated section of your local health food store. Although any kind of miso may be used for this soup, I prefer the darker red miso for its deep, earthy taste.

1. In a medium pot, heat 3$\frac{1}{2}$ cups of the water on a stove until just simmering. Remove from heat and set aside.

2. Place the miso, Nama Shoyu, ginger, and remaining $\frac{1}{2}$ cup of water in a food processor and mix until smooth. Add this mixture to the warmed water and stir until fully incorporated.

3. Ladle the soup into bowls and top with the scallions and seaweed. Let the soup sit for about 5 minutes before serving to allow the seaweed to soften.

Yield: 4 or 5 servings

4 cups water

4 tablespoons miso

2 tablespoons Nama Shoyu or tamari soy sauce

4 teaspoons grated ginger

2 cups chopped scallions

1 cup wakame seaweed

Cilantro Lime Soup

Kaffir lime leaves give this soup lots of authentic Thai flavor and aroma.

1. Place all of the ingredients except the water, jicama, and cucumber in a food processor and blend until smooth and creamy. Add the water 1 to 2 tablespoons at a time until the soup reaches the desired consistency.

2. Ladle the soup into bowls. Top each bowl with jicama and cucumber and serve.

FOR A CHANGE . . .

● Sprinkle some chopped scallions on top of each bowl.

● Dice a few shitake mushrooms, marinate in 2 tablespoons of Nama Shoyu for 1 hour, and place on top of the soup.

Yield: About 4 servings

3 kaffir lime leaves

$\frac{3}{4}$ cup raw almond butter

$\frac{1}{2}$ cup raw or untoasted sesame oil

$\frac{1}{2}$ cup chopped fresh cilantro

$\frac{1}{4}$ cup freshly squeezed lime juice

3 tablespoons Nama Shoyu, or 2 tablespoons Bragg Liquid Aminos

3 tablespoons freshly squeezed lemon juice

2 tablespoons raw honey

2 tablespoons grated ginger

1 cup water

1 cup diced jicama

1 cup diced cucumber

Yield: 15 to 20 rolls

1 clove garlic, chopped

2 cups shredded cabbage

2 cups shredded radish

1 cup shredded carrots

3 tablespoons freshly squeezed lemon juice

1 tablespoon grated ginger

1 tablespoon red miso

1 tablespoon Nama Shoyu or tamari soy sauce

1 tablespoon raw or untoasted sesame oil

15 to 20 rice spring roll wrappers

$\frac{1}{2}$ cup finely sliced red bell peppers

$\frac{1}{2}$ cup thinly sliced cucumber

1 $\frac{1}{2}$ cups finely chopped fresh cilantro

$\frac{1}{2}$ cup Asian Dipping Sauce (page 105)

Paste

$\frac{1}{2}$ cup ground raw almond butter

1 teaspoon grated ginger

$\frac{1}{2}$ teaspoon cayenne pepper powder

Spring Rolls

These spring rolls are a hit at every party. My raw food and non-raw food friends alike always request these very special appetizers.

1. To make the filling, place the garlic, cabbage, radish, carrots, lemon juice, ginger, miso, Nama Shoyu, and sesame oil in a large bowl. Mix and let marinate overnight, or for 12 hours, in the refrigerator.

2. To make the paste, place the almond butter, ginger, and cayenne in the food processor and blend well to combine. Set aside.

3. Once the filling has marinated, prepare the rolls. Soften a rice wrapper by soaking it in warm water for 1 minute. Carefully remove the rice wrapper from the warm water, and place it on a cutting board. Dab it dry with a paper towel.

4. Carefully and gently spread 1 teaspoon of the paste across the bottom of the wrapper. Next, layer a spoonful of filling (be sure to drain any excess liquid), a piece of red bell pepper, a slice of cucumber, and a tablespoon of cilantro.

5. To form the spring rolls, first fold the right and left sides of the wrapper over the filling (like a burrito). Then, starting at the bottom, roll up the wrapper. (See the figures on page 97.)

6. Repeat steps 3 through 5 for the remaining wrappers.

7. Arrange the rolls seam side down on a platter, and serve with Asian Dipping Sauce.

FOR A CHANGE . . .

- Sprinkle parsley and/or sesame seeds on top of the filling before rolling the wrappers.
- Cut each roll in half and serve as a bite-sized appetizer instead of a meal.

HOW TO FORM THE SPRING ROLLS

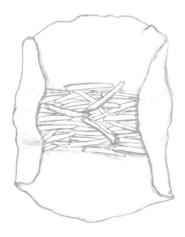

1. Fold the right and left sides of the wrapper over the filling.

2. Start at the bottom and roll the wrapper up.

Wilted Spinach Salad

This easy-to-prepare salad is so satisfying, it will quickly become a household favorite.

1. In a large bowl, combine the spinach and the dressing. Let marinate for 20 minutes at room temperature.

2. Sprinkle the sesame seeds over the top of the salad and serve.

Yield: 4 to 6 servings

- - - - - - - -

4 cups coarsely chopped spinach

$^1/_4$ cup Sesame Miso Dressing (page 99)

2 tablespoons raw or untoasted sesame seeds

FOR A CHANGE . . .

● Sprinkle any or all of the following on the top of the salad: $^1/_2$ cup diced scallions, $^1/_2$ cup diced jicama, or $^1/_2$ cup diced red or orange peppers.

Seaweed Salad

Seaweed is high in vitamins A, C, E, and K.
Many believe it to be a detoxifier and a healing agent,
as well as a protector against breast and other cancers.

Yield: 4 to 6 servings

2 cups dry dulse seaweed

2 cups dry wakame seaweed

¹/₄ cup Sweet Ginger Dressing (page 99)

Topping

¹/₄ cup raw or untoasted sesame seeds

¹/₄ cup minced scallions

1. Put both types of seaweed in a medium bowl. Add cool water to the bowl until the seaweed is just covered. Let soak for 1 hour, or until the seaweed is soft.

2. Drain the seaweed in a colander and pat it dry with a paper towel.

3. Coarsely chop the seaweed and place it back in the bowl. Toss with the dressing.

4. Sprinkle the sesame seeds and scallions over the top of the salad and serve.

FOR A CHANGE . . .

- Sprinkle 2 tablespoons black sesame seeds over the top of the salad.

Almond Ginger Dressing

This versatile and hearty dressing combines the
classic Asian flavors of almond and ginger.

Yield: About 1¹/₂ cups

³/₄ cup raw almond butter

¹/₄ cup freshly squeezed lime juice

3 tablespoons Nama Shoyu, or 2 tablespoons Bragg Liquid Aminos

2 tablespoons raw honey

2 tablespoons grated ginger

¹/₄ cup water

1. Place all of the ingredients except the water in a food processor and mix until fully combined. Add the water 1 or 2 tablespoons at a time until the desired consistency is reached. You may need to stop the food processor several times to scrape down the sides.

2. Use the dressing immediately, or transfer to a container and refrigerate until ready to use.

Sesame Miso Dressing

*This versatile dressing can give
any salad an Asian flair!*

1. Place all of the ingredients in a food processor or blender and pulse until completely combined.

2. Use the dressing immediately, or transfer to a container and refrigerate until ready to use. If refrigerating, allow the dressing to return to room temperature and stir vigorously before using.

TASTES GREAT WITH . . .

Wilted Spinach Salad (page 85) or Seaweed Salad (page 98).

FOR A CHANGE . . .

● Use other types of miso for a variety in flavor.

Yield: About 1 cup

3/4 cup raw or untoasted sesame oil

1/4 cup freshly squeezed lemon juice

2 tablespoons Nama Shoyu, or 1 1/2 tablespoons Bragg Liquid Aminos

1 tablespoon raw honey

1 teaspoon white miso

Sweet Ginger Dressing

*This slightly sweet dressing can turn any salad
into an Asian delicacy.*

1. Place all of the ingredients in a food processor or blender and pulse until completely combined.

2. Use dressing immediately, or transfer to a container and refrigerate until ready to use. If refrigerating, allow the dressing to return to room temperature and stir vigorously before using.

TASTES GREAT WITH . . .

Wilted Spinach Salad (page 85) or Spinach Salad with Pineapple and Jicama (page 114).

Yield: About 1 cup

2 cloves garlic

1/3 cup freshly squeezed lemon juice

1/3 cup raw or untoasted sesame oil

4 tablespoons Nama Shoyu, or 3 tablespoons Bragg Liquid Aminos

3 tablespoons minced ginger

2 tablespoons white miso

1 tablespoon raw honey

Sushi

Once you understand the simple technique of rolling sushi, you can make it using any vegetables you like! This is a fantastic and quick meal that the whole family will enjoy. I prefer using untoasted seaweed sheets, but toasted can be substituted.

Yield: About 6 servings

. . . .

6 sheets nori seaweed

6 leaves romaine lettuce

1 avocado, sliced into $1/8$-inch strips

$1/2$ jicama, sliced into strips $1/8$-inch wide and 2 inches long

$1/4$ red bell pepper, sliced into $1/8$-inch strips

$1/4$ cup radish sprouts (see page 30 for sprouting instructions)

$1/2$ cup Asian Dipping Sauce (page 105)

1. Place a sheet of nori on a clean flat surface with one of the longer sides closest to you. Lay a romaine lettuce leaf on the sheet lengthwise, leaving at least a $1/2$-inch border on both of the longer sides. (See Figure 1 on page 101.)

2. Place a portion of the avocado, jicama, and red bell pepper in a long, flat mound along the side of the romaine leaf that is closest to you. Top with sprouts. (See Figure 2.)

3. Starting at the side closest to you, firmly roll up the nori over the filling. Once the roll is wrapped, wet your fingers with water and press down the edges to seal. (See Figure 3.)

4. Repeat steps 1 through 3 with the remaining nori and filling.

5. Slice each roll into 4 pieces with a serrated knife. (See Figure 4.) Serve with Asian Dipping Sauce.

FOR A CHANGE . . .

● Mix $1/2$ cup chopped almonds, 1 tablespoon ginger, and 1 tablespoon Nama Shoyu in a food processor. Spread this mixture on the romaine leaves before filling and rolling the sushi.

HOW TO FORM THE SUSHI

1.

Place the nori on a flat, clean surface with one of the longer sides closest to you. Lay a romaine leaf on the sheet lengthwise, leaving at least a $1/2$-inch border on the two longer sides.

2.

Place a portion of the filling in a long mound along the bottom side of the romaine leaf. Flatten the mound as much as possible, then top with the sprouts.

3.

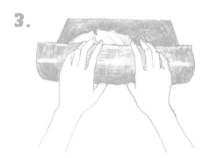

Starting with the side closest to you, roll the nori away from you. Firmly roll over the filling, trying not to let any spill out. Once the roll is completely wrapped, wet your fingers with water and press down the edges to seal them.

4.

Using a serrated knife, carefully slice each roll into four pieces. If you'd like to have more sushi, or if you are serving the sushi as an appetizer instead of a meal, you can slice each roll into five or six smaller pieces.

Pad Thai

Traditionally made with rice noodles, this raw food version uses "noodles" made from vegetables instead.

Yield: 6 to 8 servings

. . . .

2 large zucchini, peeled

$3/_4$ cup raw almond butter

$1/_4$ cup freshly squeezed lime juice

3 tablespoons Nama Shoyu, or 2 tablespoons Bragg Liquid Aminos

2 tablespoons raw honey

2 tablespoons grated ginger

2 cups mung bean sprouts, or adzuki bean sprouts

$3/_4$ cup coarsely chopped raw or untoasted almonds

1. To make the "noodles," use a spiralizer or vegetable peeler to form the zucchini into long, thin strips. Place the noodles in a colander and let sit for 20 minutes to drain their natural liquid. (This will keep the dish from becoming too watery.)

2. Place the almond butter, lime juice, Nama Shoyu, honey, and ginger in a blender or food processor and mix until combined. If the sauce is too thick, add water 1 to 2 tablespoons at a time until the desired consistency is reached.

3. In a large bowl, gently mix the noodles with the almond sauce.

4. Transfer the noodles to plates and top with the bean sprouts and almonds. Serve immediately.

FOR A CHANGE . . .

● Use yellow squash instead of, or in addition to, the zucchini when making the noodles.

● Top the finished dish with $1/_4$ cup coarsely chopped fresh cilantro and/or $1/_4$ cup grated carrots for a different appearance and taste.

FYI . . .

To get mung bean sprouts that are thick and fat requires extra time and equipment. Additionally, mung beans are not available in many supermarkets. Therefore, I recommend buying them already sprouted. However, if you would like to sprout your own, sprouting instructions are on page 30.

Daikon Dumplings

These dumplings are an amazing dish to serve if you want to impress guests at your next dinner party. They are so easy to prepare, and they simply burst with delicious Asian flavor. Don't be surprised if your friends beg you for the recipe!

1. Place the pine nuts in a food processor and pulse until completely blended. Transfer to a medium bowl.

2. Add the shallot, celery, red bell pepper, cilantro, ginger, sesame oil, and lime juice to the pine nuts and stir until combined. Set aside.

3. Using a mandolin slicer or a knife, cut the daikon into 24 to 30 thin rounds that are $\frac{1}{8}$-inch thick or less. Arrange the rounds on a serving platter.

4. To assemble the dumplings, place a spoonful of pine nut filling on top of a daikon round. Place another daikon round on top of the filling to complete the dumpling. Continue until all the daikon rounds have been used.

5. Serve and enjoy!

FOR A CHANGE . . .

● Use parsnips or jicama instead of daikon for the dumpling shell.

● Drizzle the dumplings with sesame oil and/or Nama Shoyu.

● Use cookie cutters to cut the daikon rounds into fun shapes—this is a great way to get kids involved in the preparation of this meal!

Yield: 12 to 15 dumplings

$\frac{1}{2}$ cup raw or untoasted pine nuts

1 shallot, diced

1 stalk celery, finely diced

$\frac{1}{2}$ red bell pepper, diced

$\frac{1}{4}$ cup dried cilantro

2 tablespoons grated ginger

2 tablespoons raw or untoasted sesame oil

1 tablespoon freshly squeezed lime juice

1 large daikon, peeled

Yield: 4 to 6 servings

. . . .

1 cup broccoli florets, chopped
into $1/2$-inch pieces

$1/2$ cup diced red onion

3 tablespoons freshly squeezed
lemon juice

1 teaspoon sea salt

12-ounce packet of kelp noodles
(see page 23)

Curry Sauce

2 avocados, peeled

2 kaffir lime leaves

$1/4$ cup freshly squeezed
orange juice

3 tablespoons freshly squeezed
lemon juice

1 tablespoon grated ginger

1 teaspoon curry powder

1 teaspoon sea salt

$1/2$ teaspoon chili powder

Kelp Noodles with Green Curry Sauce

*Kelp noodles are clear, mild-tasting noodles that are
made up of 100 percent seaweed. When paired with
curry sauce, they make a fantastic meal—
especially when you are craving carbohydrates.*

1. Place the broccoli, onion, lemon juice, and salt in a
medium bowl. Mix, then let marinate for 1 hour at room
temperature.

2. To make the sauce, place all of the sauce ingredients in
a food processor and mix until completely smooth. If the
consistency is too thick, add water 1 or 2 tablespoons at a
time until the desired consistency is reached. Set aside.

3. Rinse the kelp noodles in cold water. Drain them in a
colander, then transfer to a large bowl.

4. Pour the sauce over the noodles and mix. Sprinkle the
marinated broccoli and onion over the top and serve.

FOR A CHANGE . . .

● Use pineapple juice instead of orange juice.

● Sprinkle a few tablespoons of dried coconut on top of
the finished meal for an exotic taste.

Marinated Ginger Cabbage

*This dish is extremely easy to prepare
and serves as a flavorful addition to any Asian meal.*

1. In a medium bowl, combine the water, miso, ginger, lemon juice, Nama Shoyu, and vinegar. Stir in the cabbage and let marinate for at least 2 hours at room temperature.

2. Serve immediately, or refrigerate until ready to serve.

FOR A CHANGE . . .

- Use red cabbage, grated carrots, baby bok choy, or napa cabbage in addition to or in place of the green cabbage.
- Use other types of miso for a variety in flavor.

Yield: 6 to 8 servings

- - - - - - - -

$1/4$ cup water

2 tablespoons red miso

2 tablespoons grated ginger

2 tablespoons freshly squeezed lemon juice

2 tablespoons Nama Shoyu or tamari soy sauce

1 tablespoon apple cider vinegar

1 head of green cabbage, shredded fine

Asian Dipping Sauce

*This versatile dipping sauce can be paired
with just about any Asian appetizer.*

1. Place all of the ingredients in a food processor or blender and mix until fully combined.

2. Serve immediately, or transfer to a container and refrigerate until ready to use.

TASTES GREAT WITH . . .

Spring Rolls (page 96), Sushi (page 100), or freshly cut vegetables.

Yield: About $1/2$ cup

- - - - - - - -

4 tablespoons freshly squeezed lemon juice

4 tablespoons Nama Shoyu or tamari soy sauce

2 tablespoons raw or untoasted sesame oil

2 teaspoons finely chopped ginger

1 teaspoon white miso

1 teaspoon raw honey

Pineapple with Ginger Chocolate Fondue

This is a real hit at every party, and eating it won't make you feel like you have to hit the gym hard the next day!

Yield: 4 to 6 servings

1 cup dates

2 cups water

$^1/_4$ cup raw honey

1 cup cacao powder

1 tablespoon grated ginger

1 whole pineapple

1. Place the dates in the water and let soak for 1 hour, or until soft. Reserving the soak water, drain the dates and place them in a medium bowl.

2. Add the honey and $^1/_2$ cup of the soaking water to the dates. Mix to combine.

3. To make the fondue, place the dates, cacao, and ginger in the food processor and mix until smooth and creamy. Set aside.

4. To prepare the pineapple, lay it on its side and cut off about $^1/_2$-inch from the top and bottom so that it can stand flat. (See Figure 1 on page 107.)

5. Stand the pineapple on a cutting board. Using a sharp knife, carefully remove the hard exterior, cutting from top to bottom. (See Figure 2.)

6. Cut the pineapple in half lengthwise, then cut each piece in half lengthwise once again. Remove the core from each piece, then cut each piece into 1-inch slices. (See Figure 3.)

7. Arrange the pineapple around the fondue dip. Use forks to dip the pineapple in the fondue and enjoy!

FOR A CHANGE . . .

● For a fancier serving option, use wooden skewers to dip the pineapple in the fondue instead of forks—especially if you're serving the fondue at a party.

● Instead of pineapple, dip orange sections, thinly sliced Asian pears, jicama slices, or raw or untoasted cashews into the fondue.

HOW TO CORE A PINEAPPLE

1.

Lay the pineapple on its side. Using a sharp knife, cut about $\frac{1}{2}$ inch off the top and bottom of the pineapple so that it can stand flat.

2.

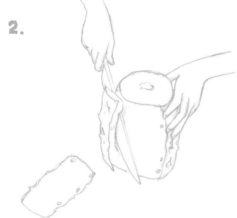

Stand the pineapple up on a cutting board or counter. Cutting from top to bottom, carefully remove the pineapple's hard exterior.

3.

With the pineapple still standing, cut it in half lengthwise from top to bottom. Cut each piece in half lengthwise once again so you are left with four long pieces. Remove the core from each piece and then cut the pieces into 1-inch slices.

Almond Cookies

Contrary to traditional almond cookies, which are filled with partially hydrogenated oil, these cookies are healthy—and bursting with flavor.

Yield: 12 to 15 cookies

. . . .

1 cup oat groats

3 cups water

1/2 cup dates

1 cup raw almond butter

2 teaspoons organic almond extract

1 cup raw or untoasted whole almonds

1. Place the groats in 2 cups of the water and let them soak overnight, or for 12 hours. Rinse and drain the groats, then place them in a food processor.

2. Place the dates in the remaining 1 cup of water and let soak for 1 hour, or until soft. Drain the dates and place them in the food processor with the groats.

3. Add the almond butter and almond extract to the food processor and mix until smooth.

4. Drop the dough by rounded teaspoons onto Teflex dehydrator sheets. Press 3 almonds into each ball of dough.

5. Place the sheets in a dehydrator and dehydrate at 105°F for 24 to 36 hours, or until desired crunchiness is reached. (If you don't own a dehydrator, see page 5 for instructions on how to use an oven for this purpose.) Remove and serve.

FOR A CHANGE . . .

● Sprinkle any or all of the following on top of the cookies before dehydrating: cacao nibs, crushed almonds, or dried coconut.

FYI . . .

Studies have reported that almonds may help lower LDL (bad) cholesterol.

6

Caribbean Raw Cuisine

The bold, bright flavors of Caribbean cuisine are highlighted in the following recipes, which have been adapted from all over the equatorial region. In this chapter, I have included both classic and exciting new Caribbean cuisine that is fresh, flavorful, and exotic. When you prepare any of these treats, you will be transported to the warm Caribbean beaches, even on the coldest of winter days.

Be sure to look at the next page for menu ideas for both a simple Caribbean meal and an elegant Caribbean feast. Regardless of the amount of time you have to prepare, you will be able to bring the delicious flavors of the Caribbean to your home.

Menu Ideas

The sample menus on this page will allow you to create delicious raw Caribbean meals, regardless of the amount of time you can dedicate to preparation. The simple, quick meal can be prepared and served immediately. However, if you have time to spare, I recommend the elegant feast. For both menus, the flavors of each dish complement each other beautifully, awakening the senses and allowing you and your guests to enjoy a healthy Caribbean meal. Preparation time approximations have been given for the elegant feast, so you can prepare it with ease without feeling rushed.

A Simple and Quick Caribbean Meal
(Prepare right before serving)

Spinach Salad with Jicama and Pineapple in a Caribbean Lime Dressing

Sweet Potato Stew

Banana Mango Cream Pie

An Elegant Feast
(Requires extra time and equipment)

Conch Fritters with Mustard Sauce
(begin the day before to dehydrate)

Curried Roti with Peas and Sweet Potatoes
(begin the day before to dehydrate)

Coconut Ice Cream with Banana Crumble
(make at least 4 hours ahead to freeze)

Mango Soup With Sweet Cashew Cream

This soup is so versatile, it can be served as either a fantastic starter or a delicious dessert. Plus, the taste is out of this world.

1. To make the cream, place the cashews in a food processor and pulse until completely blended. Add the water, honey, and lemon juice and mix until creamy. Transfer to a medium bowl and set aside. You may need to stop the food processor several times to scrape down the sides.

2. For the soup, place the mangos, lemon juice, and honey in a food processor and pulse until completely smooth. Slowly add the cashew cream to the food processor and mix until thoroughly combined.

3. Transfer the soup to bowls and serve.

FOR A CHANGE . . .

● Top the soup with $1/4$ cup raw cashews or $1/4$ cup finely diced mango before serving.

Yield: About 4 cups

2 ripe mangos, peeled

2 tablespoons freshly squeezed lemon juice

I tablespoon raw honey

Sweet Cashew Cream

I cup raw or untoasted cashews

3 tablespoons water

I tablespoon raw honey

I tablespoon freshly squeezed lemon juice

TIP . . .

Always wash mangos before peeling, as the skin may harbor bacteria and/or pesticide residue.

"Conch" Fritters

Using jicama and peaches in place of the traditional Caribbean conch gives this dish a healthy twist. These delicious fritters require a little bit of extra time to prepare, but they are worth it!

Yield: 8 to 10 fritters

- - - - - - - - - -

4 scallions,
coarsely chopped

2 cups fresh corn,
or frozen and thawed

I cup flax seeds

I cup chopped fresh cilantro

I teaspoon dried coriander

I teaspoon sea salt

I cup finely diced jicama

I cup finely diced peaches

1. Place the scallions, corn, flax seeds, cilantro, coriander, and salt in a food processor. Pulse until the ingredients are mixed, but a little chunky.

2. Transfer the mixture to a medium bowl and add the jicama and peaches. Stir to combine.

3. With wet hands, form the batter into slightly flattened balls about $2\frac{1}{2}$ inches in diameter (they should look like large balls of cookie dough). Place the balls on Teflex dehydrator sheets and dehydrate at 105°F for 12 to 24 hours, or until the fritters appear slightly crunchy. (If you don't own a dehydrator, see page 5 for instructions on how to use an oven for this purpose.)

4. Arrange the fritters on a platter and serve with either Mustard Sauce (page 113) or Mango Salsa (page 113).

FOR A CHANGE . . .

- Use mangos instead of peaches for a different flavor.

Mango Salsa

This fresh salsa serves as a fantastic accompaniment to any Caribbean meal.

1. Place all of the ingredients in a large bowl and stir to combine. Let marinate for 30 minutes at room temperature.

2. Use immediately, or refrigerate until ready to use.

TASTES GREAT WITH . . .

"Conch" Fritters (page 112) or Roti (page 120).

Yield: About 2 cups

I large mango, diced

$1/4$ cup finely diced red onion

$1/4$ cup diced cucumber

$1/4$ cup finely diced fresh cilantro

$1/4$ cup diced jicama

3 tablespoons freshly squeezed lime juice

I teaspoon finely diced jalapeño pepper

$1/8$ teaspoon sea salt

Mustard Sauce

This creamy sauce is a great accompaniment to many meals. My favorite dishes to pair it with are "Conch" Fritters and Roti.

1. Place the cashews in a food processor and grind until they are well-blended. Add all of the remaining ingredients and blend until smooth and creamy. If the mixture is too thick, add water 1 or 2 tablespoons at a time to thin it down.

2. Use the sauce immediately, or transfer to a container and refrigerate until ready to use. If refrigerating, allow the sauce to return to room temperature and stir vigorously before serving.

Yield: About I cup

$1/2$ cup raw or untoasted cashews

2 cloves garlic

$1/4$ cup chopped fresh cilantro

$1/4$ cup cold pressed extra virgin olive oil

2 tablespoons freshly squeezed lime juice

I teaspoon ground mustard seed

I teaspoon sea salt

Spinach Salad with Jicama and Pineapple

When combined, the contrasting tastes of sweet pineapple and earthy spinach result in a wonderfully flavorful salad.

Yield: 4 to 6 servings

4 cups coarsely chopped baby spinach leaves

1 cup Caribbean Lime Dressing (page 116)

¹/₂ cup sliced jicama (¹/₄-inch strips)

¹/₂ cup fresh pineapple cubes (about 1 inch)

¹/₄ cup chopped fresh cilantro

1. In a large bowl, toss the spinach leaves with the dressing.

2. Sprinkle the jicama, pineapple, and cilantro over the top of the salad and serve immediately.

FOR A CHANGE . . .

● Use orange slices instead of pineapple cubes.

● Sprinkle coarsely chopped raw almonds over the top of the salad before serving.

● Allow the spinach to marinate in the dressing for 30 minutes before adding the topping for a wilted, slightly crunchy salad.

Avocado, Mango, and Melon Salad

This salad is an excellent starter to a festive meal, but it also works great as a quick and light summer lunch.

1. Cut each melon in half and scoop out the seeds. (The four halves will serve as bowls.) Set aside for later.

2. Place the rest of the ingredients in a medium bowl and mix gently by hand to combine.

3. Distribute the mixture evenly into the melon bowls. Serve immediately.

FOR A CHANGE . . .

● Experiment with different varieties of melon, such as casaba, Galia, canteloupe, crenshaw, or Tokyo King.

Yield: 4 servings

2 honeydew melons

2 mangos, peeled and cut into $1/2$-inch cubes

1 avocado, peeled and cut into $1/2$-inch cubes

$1/4$ red onion, finely diced

$1/4$ jicama, diced ($1/2$-inch cubes)

$1/4$ cup cold pressed extra virgin olive oil

$1/4$ cup freshly squeezed lime juice

2 tablespoons chopped fresh mint leaves

$1/2$ teaspoon red chili flakes

Pinch sea salt

TIP . . .

If after scooping out the seeds the melon bowl seems too shallow to hold the filling, simply use a spoon or ice cream scoop to scoop out some of the melon flesh, creating a deeper bowl.

Caribbean Lime Dressing

Yield: About 1 1/2 cups

. . . .

1 cup fresh pineapple cubes

1/4 cup raw or untoasted sesame oil

2 tablespoons chopped shallot

2 tablespoons freshly squeezed lime juice

2 tablespoons chopped fresh Italian parsley

1 teaspoon sea salt

1/2 teaspoon red chili pepper flakes

The inspiration for this dressing came to me while I was traveling through the Caribbean. One taste will transport you to a tropical island!

1. Place all of the ingredients in a food processor and blend until smooth. If necessary, add water 1 to 2 tablespoons at a time until the desired consistency is reached.

2. Use immediately, or transfer to a container and refrigerate until ready to use. If refrigerating, allow the dressing to return to room temperature and stir vigorously before serving.

Pomegranate Honey Vinaigrette

Yield: About 1 cup

. . . .

4 tablespoons freshly squeezed pomegranate juice

4 tablespoons raw honey

1/2 cup balsamic vinegar

1/2 cup cold pressed extra virgin olive oil

1 teaspoon sea salt

This dressing is a great way to dress up any salad and give it an exotic flair. Not only does the pomegranate juice taste delicious, it is rich in antioxidants and a great immune system booster. If possible, use freshly squeezed juice. (See page 7 for juicing instructions.)

1. Place all of the ingredients in a food processor and blend until smooth. If necessary, add water 1 or 2 tablespoons at a time until the desired consistency is reached.

2. Use the dressing immediately, or transfer to a container and refrigerate until ready to use. If refrigerating, allow the dressing to return to room temperature and stir vigorously before serving.

Sweet Potato Stew

*This hearty, satisfying stew
is so simple to prepare.*

1. In a blender or food processor, combine all of the soup ingredients until smooth and creamy.

2. Ladle the soup into bowls. Top each serving with a generous portion of Asian pear and peas and serve.

FOR A CHANGE . . .

● Try adding any of the following toppings to the soup: peeled and diced Granny Smith apples, diced scallions, chopped cilantro, or fresh corn kernels.

FYI . . .

One sweet potato contains almost twice the Recommended Daily Allowance (RDA) of vitamin A.

Yield: About 4 cups

3 carrots, peeled and roughly chopped

2 cloves garlic

1/2 large orange sweet potato, peeled and diced (about 1 cup)

1/2 cup water

1/2 cup raw almond butter

3 tablespoons freshly squeezed lemon juice

2 tablespoons raw honey

1 tablespoon raw or untoasted coconut oil

1/2 teaspoon sea salt

1/2 teaspoon ground cinnamon

Topping

1 Asian pear, diced into 1-inch cubes (about 1 cup)

1 cup fresh peas

"Whitefish" Melon

By cutting the melon into the rough shape of a filet and marinating it,
the melon takes on the essence of whitefish. Adding mango salsa transforms
this meal into a terrific Caribbean treat. Personally, I think casaba melons
taste best with this recipe, but honeydew melons can be substituted.

Yield: 4 to 6 servings

2 ripe white flesh melons

1 clove garlic, chopped

1 tablespoon raw honey

2 teaspoons freshly
squeezed lemon juice

$1/_8$ teaspoon sea salt

1 cup Mango Salsa (page 113)

1. Using a knife, peel the skin from both melons, then cut them in half crosswise. Scoop out and discard the seeds. (See Figure 1 below.)

2. With a knife, slice through each melon half horizontally to separate the top rounded "dome" portion. (See Figure 2 on page 119.) Keep these domed pieces and reserve the rest of the melon for another use.

3. Place the four rounded domes cut side down on the counter, then cut each one into thirds for a total of 12 pieces. (See Figure 3.) These will be your "filets."

4. Cut lines into each piece to resemble the scales of a fish. (See Figure 4.)

5. In a medium bowl, combine the garlic, honey, lemon juice, and salt. Add the filets, making sure each one is coated, and let marinate for 4 hours in the refrigerator.

6. Remove the filets and allow them to sit for 30 minutes at room temperature. Place a scoop of Mango Salsa on each filet, and serve.

HOW TO FILET AND MARINATE A MELON

1.

Using a knife, peel the skin from both of the melons. Cut both of the melons in half crosswise. Using a spoon or ice cream scoop, remove and discard the seeds.

2.

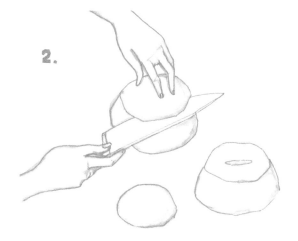

Carefully slice through each of the four halves horizontally to separate the top rounded "dome" portion from the rest of the melon. Keep the domes and reserve the rest of the melon for another use.

3.

Place the four domes cut side down on a cutting board or counter. Cut each dome into three pieces for a total of twelve pieces. These will be your fish "filets."

4.

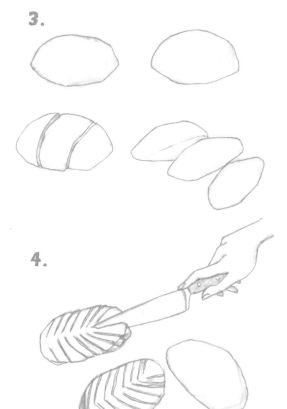

Cut lines into each of the filets to resemble the scales of a fish. Or, get creative and use the knife to carve your own design into each of the filets!

Roti with Curried Pea and Sweet Potato Filling

Yield: 4 to 6 servings

Roti

4 scallions

2 cloves garlic

2 stalks celery

2 cups sprouted wheat berries
(see page 30 for sprouting
instructions)

I cup ground flax seeds

I cup roughly chopped red
bell pepper

$\frac{1}{2}$ cup chopped red onion

$\frac{1}{4}$ teaspoon sea salt

Filling

2 cloves garlic

I medium sweet potato, peeled
and roughly chopped

I orange, peeled and sectioned

$\frac{1}{2}$ cup dried coconut

2 tablespoons grated ginger

$\frac{1}{2}$ teaspoon curry powder

$\frac{1}{8}$ teaspoon sea salt

3 scallions, chopped

I cup fresh peas, or frozen
and thawed

*Traditional roti consists of bread wrapped around
curried potatoes and peas. For this raw adaptation,
the bread is replaced by wheat berries and flax seeds,
leaving the finished product much healthier.
Make sure you start preparing these early in the day
so that you can serve them warm at dinnertime.*

1. Place all of the roti ingredients in a food processor and mix until smooth.

2. Form the mixture into circles that are approximately 4 inches in diameter and $\frac{1}{4}$ inch thick. Place the circles on Teflex dehydrator sheets and dehydrate at 105°F for 4 to 6 hours or until the crusts are firm, but pliable. (If you don't own a dehydrator, see page 5 for instructions on how to use an oven for this purpose.)

3. While the rotis are dehydrating, prepare the filling by placing all of the filling ingredients except the scallions and peas in a food processor and blending until smooth. Transfer to a large bowl and gently stir in the scallions and peas.

4. When the rotis are ready, add a scoop of the filling to the center of each crust, then fold them in half so they resemble tacos. With wet fingers, press the edges together to seal the filling inside.

5. Return the filled rotis to the dehydrator and dehydrate for an additional 4 hours, or until they are firm to the touch.

6. Serve as is, or pair with Mustard Sauce (page 113) and/or Mango Salsa (page 113).

Caribbean Spinach Bisque

This soup is chock full of more vitamins and minerals than you can imagine! Bursting with flavor and powerful antioxidants, it is sure to become a household staple.

1. Place the walnuts in the food processor and pulse until completely chopped. Add the remaining ingredients and mix until smooth and creamy.

2. Ladle the soup into bowls and top with the cucumber. Serve.

Yield: About 4 servings

1 cup walnuts

1 head watercress, leaves roughly chopped (about 1 cup)

4 cups baby spinach leaves (about 6 ounces)

1/2 cup water

1/2 cup chopped fresh cilantro

1/4 cup freshly squeezed lemon juice

1 tablespoon virgin coconut oil

1 tablespoon chopped ginger root

1/2 teaspoon sea salt

Topping

1 cup peeled, diced cucumber

Banana Mango Cream Pie

Yield: 8-inch pie

. . . .

Crust

$1/2$ cup dates

I cup water

I cup raw or untoasted cashews

I cup raw or untoasted walnuts

I teaspoon organic vanilla extract

Filling

$1/2$ cup raw or untoasted cashews

2 ripe mangos, peeled and cut
into chunks

2 ripe bananas, peeled and cut
into chunks

$1/2$ cup dried mango slices, soaked
in warm water for 5 minutes

$1/2$ cup dried coconut flakes

I teaspoon organic vanilla extract

This pie is so simple to prepare, and the taste is out of this world. The flavors are light and tropical, and you can't beat how healthy you feel after eating it!

1. Place the dates in the water and let soak for 1 hour, or until soft. Reserving the soaking liquid, drain the dates and set them aside.

2. To make the crust, place the cashews and walnuts in a food processor and chop until completely ground. Add the dates and vanilla and pulse until fully combined. If necessary, add the reserved soaking liquid 1 or 2 tablespoons at a time until the crust has a cookie dough-like consistency.

3. Transfer the mixture to an 8-inch springform or pie pan (springform pans work best because the sides are removable) and press it evenly and firmly on the bottom and side.

4. To make the filling, place the cashews in a food processor and finely chop. Add the mangos, bananas, soaked dried mango (be sure to drain before adding), coconut, and vanilla, and pulse until the filling is completely smooth, scraping down the sides if necessary.

5. Pour the filling into the crust. Place the pie in the refrigerator and let it set for at least 1 hour. Serve chilled.

FOR A CHANGE . . .

● Add diced bananas and dried coconut to the top of the pie for a decorative and delicious finish.

Mango Ice Pops

These pops are so easy to make,
and they are a great healthy dessert to serve kids.

1. Peel the mangos and place them in a blender or food processor along with the honey and blend until smooth. Add the water 1 to 2 tablespoons at a time until the consistency is thick and creamy. You may not need to use all the water.

2. Pour the mixture into ice pop molds, ice cube trays, or paper cups. Insert a wooden stick into each pop and place in the freezer.

3. Once the ice pops are frozen, pull them out by the stick and serve!

FOR A CHANGE . . .

● Add $1/2$ cup frozen peach, $1/2$ cup pineapple chunks, or $1/2$ cup diced papaya to the mixture before blending for different taste sensations.

● Add $1/2$ teaspoon ground cardamom or $1/2$ teaspoon ground cinnamon to the mixture before placing it in the freezer.

● Omit the sticks and drop mango ice cubes into sparkling water for a delicious drink.

Yield: About 6 ice pops, or 1 tray of ice cube pops

. . . .

3 ripe mangos,
or 4 cups frozen mango

3 tablespoons raw honey

$1/4$ cup water

Yield: 4 to 6 servings

· · · · · · · ·

1 cup raw or untoasted
cashews

$^1/_2$ cup raw or untoasted
pine nuts

1 cup dried coconut flakes
(preferably organic)

1 cup water

3 tablespoons raw honey

2 teaspoons organic vanilla
extract

Banana Crumble

$^1/_4$ cup raw oats

$^1/_4$ cup raw or untoasted
cashews

2 bananas, peeled and diced

$^1/_2$ cup raisins

2 teaspoons raw honey

1 teaspoon ground cinnamon

Coconut Ice Cream with Banana Crumble

This is by far one of the easiest and creamiest ice cream recipes. You don't even need an ice cream maker or high-speed blender to make it, and the end result is delicious!

1. Place the cashews and pine nuts in a food processor and chop until completely ground. Add the coconut, water, honey, and vanilla, and combine until the mixture is very well-blended.

2. Scoop the mixture into a container and place in the freezer for 3 to 4 hours, or until frozen. (Tempered glass jars with lids, such as Mason or jam jars, work well, as they freeze faster.)

3. To make the crumble, place the oats and the cashews in the food processor and pulse until the mixture resembles coarse crumbs. Transfer the mixture to a large bowl and by hand, gently mix in the bananas, raisins, honey, and cinnamon.

4. Scoop the frozen ice cream into serving bowls, top with the banana crumble, and serve.

FOR A CHANGE . . .

- Drizzle Ginger Chocolate Fondue (page 106) over the top of each serving.

South American Raw Cuisine

From the subtle flavors of ceviche to the smoky tastes of black bean soup, the food in this chapter represents the very best that South America has to offer. After living and working in Venezuela for several years and traveling around much of South America, I rejoiced in the exotic flavors and textures of the region's cuisine. However, much of traditional South American food is often fried or full of sugar. I have written this chapter to celebrate all of the beautiful flavors without sacrificing health. I hope that you enjoy eating these dishes as much as I enjoyed creating them!

Additionally, the sample menus on the next page will guide you in preparing both simple, quick meals and elegant, more elaborate feasts.

Menu Ideas

While any of the dishes in this chapter can be served together as a delicious South American meal, the following menus are intended to take the guesswork out of determining which courses work best together and how long they will take to prepare. For both menus on this page, the flavors of each dish complement each other beautifully, awakening the senses and allowing you and your guests to enjoy a healthy South American meal. Estimated preparation times have been provided, so you know what to expect before you start "cooking."

A Simple and Quick South American Meal
(Prepare right before serving)

Brazilian Cucumber Salad

Sopa de Ajo

Banana Pineapple Sorbet

An Elegant Feast
(Requires extra time and equipment)

Quinoa Salad
(begin three days before to sprout the quinoa)

Ceviche with Chimichurri Sauce
(begin the day before to marinate)

Cocadas
(begin the day before to dehydrate)

Sopa de Ajo

This classic garlic soup has origins in Spain, but is widely served throughout South America as well. For this recipe, I've added a tomato topping. Also, thinly sliced jicama is used in place of wheat bread, which is usually placed on top of each serving. I recommend using a mandolin slicer to cut the jicama, but a sharp knife can be substituted.

1. To make the topping, place the tomatoes, lemon juice, olive oil, and salt in a medium bowl. Mix gently, then let marinate for 15 minutes at room temperature.

2. Place all of the soup ingredients except the sliced jicama in a blender and combine until completely smooth.

3. Ladle the soup into bowls. Place a slice of the jicama and a spoonful of the marinated tomatoes on top of each bowl and serve.

FOR A CHANGE . . .

● Add $\frac{1}{2}$ cup chopped scallions and $\frac{1}{2}$ chopped fresh cilantro to the topping before allowing it to marinate.

Yield: 4 to 5 servings

4 cloves garlic

2 stalks celery

$\frac{1}{2}$ sweet onion, chopped (about $\frac{1}{4}$ cup)

I cup chopped jicama

$\frac{1}{2}$ cup water

$\frac{1}{4}$ cup cold pressed extra virgin olive oil

3 tablespoons freshly squeezed lemon juice

I teaspoon sea salt

$\frac{1}{2}$ jicama, peeled and sliced into $\frac{1}{8}$-inch thin rounds

Topping

I cup quartered cherry tomatoes

I tablespoon freshly squeezed lemon juice

I tablespoon cold pressed extra virgin olive oil

$\frac{1}{2}$ teaspoon sea salt

Black "Bean" Soup

Yield: About 4 cups

Black "Beans"

1 cup sunflower seeds

4 cups cool water

1 cup sun-dried tomatoes

1/4 cup chopped fresh cilantro

1/2 teaspoon chipotle chili powder

1/2 teaspoon red chili pepper flakes

Soup

1 cup sun-dried tomatoes

2 cups water

2 stalks celery, chopped

2 cloves garlic, chopped

1 medium carrot, chopped

1/2 cup chopped fresh cilantro

2 tablespoons freshly squeezed lemon juice

2 tablespoons chopped fresh thyme

1/2 teaspoon sea salt

1/2 teaspoon chipotle pepper

1/2 teaspoon chili pepper powder

1 cup diced fresh tomatoes

Beans are a staple in many South American dishes. This soup, which uses soaked sunflower seeds to make the beans, is easier to digest than traditional black bean soup—but it remains every bit as filling and delicious.

1. To prepare the "beans," place the sunflower seeds in 2 cups of the water and let soak for 4 hours. Drain and rinse the seeds and set them aside.

2. Place the sun-dried tomatoes in the remaining 2 cups of water and let soak for 1 hour, or until soft. Reserving the soaking water, drain the tomatoes and place them in a food processor.

3. Add the seeds to the food processor and pulse until the mixture is well-blended, but still chunky.

4. Transfer the bean mixture to a large bowl. Add the cilantro, chipotle chili powder, red chili pepper flakes, and 1/2 cup of the reserved tomato water. Stir to combine, then set aside while you prepare the soup.

5. To make the soup, place the sun-dried tomatoes in the water and let soak for 1 hour, or until soft. Reserving the soak water, drain the tomatoes and transfer them to a blender. Add 1 1/2 cups of the reserved water and all of the remaining soup ingredients except the fresh tomatoes and blend until smooth and creamy.

6. Transfer the soup to a large pot. Add the fresh tomatoes and the bean mixture to the soup and gently mix to combine. Ladle the soup into bowls and serve.

FOR A CHANGE . . .

• If you prefer warm soup, place the soup pot in the dehydrator at 105°F for 1 hour before serving.

• Sprinkle chopped fresh cilantro, scallions, diced avocado, and/or diced red bell pepper over the top of the soup.

• Mix some diced shallots and/or scallions with Cashew "Cheese" (page 53) and pour over the soup for a "sour cream" experience.

Gazpacho

This soup, which originated in Spain, is served widely throughout South America as well. The fresh, light ingredients are bursting with so much flavor, it will quickly become a family favorite.

1. Place 2 cups of the chopped tomatoes in a food processor (set the remaining cup aside). Add the garlic, parsley, cilantro, olive oil, lemon juice, and salt and chop until completely smooth and combined.

2. Add the remaining chopped tomato and the red bell pepper to the soup, and pulse to incorporate. The final consistency of the soup should be smooth, but a little chunky.

3. Ladle the soup into bowls. Sprinkle the avocado, cucumber, and cilantro over the top and serve.

Yield: About 4 cups

5 large tomatoes, coarsely chopped (about 3 cups)

2 cloves garlic

$1/2$ cup chopped fresh Italian parsley

$1/2$ cup chopped fresh cilantro

$1/4$ cup cold pressed extra virgin olive oil

3 tablespoons freshly squeezed lemon juice

$1/2$ teaspoon sea salt

1 cup coarsely chopped red bell pepper

Topping

1 avocado, finely diced

1 cup finely diced cucumber

1 cup chopped fresh cilantro

Tomatillo Salsa

Yield: About 1 1/2 cups

- 1 cup diced tomatillos
- 1/4 cup finely chopped fresh cilantro
- 2 tablespoons freshly squeezed lemon juice
- 1/4 teaspoon sea salt

A tomatillo is a light, refreshing green tomato. Using them for this recipe puts an exciting twist on traditional salsa. Be sure to remove the husk (outer layer) and wash the sticky substance off of the tomatillos before preparing.

1. Place all of the ingredients in a medium bowl and combine. Let marinate for 15 minutes at room temperature.

2. Serve as is, or refrigerate until ready to serve.

TASTES GREAT WITH . . .

Arepas (page 131), Quinoa Salad (below), or Spinach and Dandelion Tart (page 136).

Quinoa Salad

Yield: 4 to 6 servings

- 3 cloves garlic, diced
- 2 red bell peppers, diced
- 3 cups sprouted quinoa (see page 30 for sprouting instructions)
- 1 cup chopped fresh cilantro
- 1/2 cup cold pressed extra virgin olive oil
- 6 tablespoons freshly squeezed lemon juice
- 1 teaspoon sea salt

Referred to as the "mother grain" by the Incas, quinoa has been around for millennia. It is particularly high in protein and calcium, and has a fantastic nutty flavor. This salad is both filling and refreshing, sure to satisfy the hungriest of appetites.

1. Place all of the ingredients in a large bowl and stir by hand to combine. Let marinate for 1 hour at room temperature.

2. Transfer to salad bowls, serve, and enjoy!

FOR A CHANGE . . .

- Before transferring to bowls, top the salad with 1 cup diced avocado and/or 1 cup diced tomato.

Arepas with Tomatillo Salsa

Resembling thick, round pieces of corn bread, arepas are typical Venezuelan fare. In this recipe, I have filled them with a delightful tomatillo salsa for a fresh, light treat.

Yield: 4 arepas

. . . .

$1/_2$ cup sunflower seeds

I cup water

2 green onions, chopped

$2^1/_2$ cups fresh corn kernels, or frozen and thawed

I cup ground flax seeds

$1/_2$ cup water

$1/_2$ cup chopped fresh cilantro

$1/_2$ teaspoon red chili flakes

$1/_2$ teaspoon sea salt

$1/_2$ cup Tomatillo Salsa (page 130)

1. Place the sunflower seeds in a bowl. Add the water and let soak for 4 hours. Drain and rinse.

2. Place the drained seeds and all of the remaining ingredients except the Tomatillo Salsa in a food processor and chop until smooth.

3. Form the mixture into 8 flat circles, no more than $1/_4$-inch thick. Arrange the circles on Teflex sheets and dehydrate at 105°F for 4 hours, then flip each circle over. (If you don't own a dehydrator, see page 5 for instructions on how to use an oven for this purpose.) If the circles are still gooey or stick to the Teflex sheets, dehydrate 1 additional hour and try flipping again. Continue as necessary until the circles can be easily flipped.

4. Once flipped, remove the Teflex sheets from the dehydrator and spoon about 2 tablespoons of Tomatillo Salsa evenly on 4 of the circles. Place the remaining 4 circles on top of the salsa. With wet fingers, gently seal the edges, closing the salsa inside.

5. Return the filled arepas to the dehydrator and dehydrate for another 4 to 8 hours, or until the desired crunchiness is reached. Remove from the dehydrator and serve.

TASTES GREAT WITH . . .

Guacamole (page 66) or Green Onion Sauce (page 134).

Brazilian Cucumber Salad

This Brazilian salad is typically made with chayote—a squash found in Brazil—and hot malagueta peppers. For this version, I use cucumbers and jalapeños, which are more widely available. You can even use the avocado flesh to make guacamole, which will turn this side dish into a delicious light lunch.

Yield: 4 servings

2 medium avocados, preferably Haas

4 cucumbers, peeled and diced

$1/2$ jalapeño pepper, seeded and finely diced

$1/2$ cup South American Marinade (page 140)

1. Cut each avocado in half and scoop out the flesh. Discarding the pit, set the flesh and the 4 shells aside.

2. Place the cucumbers, pepper, and South American Marinade in a medium bowl and mix gently to combine. Let marinate for 1 hour at room temperature.

3. Scoop the marinated cucumber into the avocado shells and serve.

TIP . . .

Don't throw away the flesh! Set it aside and use it to make Guacamole (page 66) or any other recipe that requires avocado.

Chilean Tomato Salad

*This simple, delicious salad
is typically served throughout Chile.*

Yield: 4 servings

- - - - - - - -

$1/2$ medium sweet
onion, thinly sliced
(about $1/2$ cup)

$1/4$ cup cold pressed extra
virgin olive oil

3 tablespoons freshly
squeezed lemon juice

I teaspoon sea salt

4 medium fresh tomatoes,
cut into $1/4$ inch wedges

I cup chopped fresh
cilantro

1. Place the onion, olive oil, lemon juice, and salt in a medium bowl and mix to combine. Let marinate for 2 hours at room temperature to allow the onion to soften.

2. Add the tomatoes and cilantro to the onions and mix. Serve at room temperature.

FOR A CHANGE . . .

● Sprinkle $1/4$ cup chopped kalamata olives, 1 teaspoon red chili pepper flakes, and/or $1/2$ teaspoon cumin powder over the top of the salad.

Creamy Cumin and Avocado Dressing

Yield: About 2 cups

- - - - - - -

I ripe avocado

I clove garlic

$3/4$ cup freshly squeezed
lemon juice

$1/4$ cup chopped fresh
cilantro

I teaspoon sea salt

I teaspoon ground cumin

This dressing, which is both creamy and smoky, serves as a hearty topping for any salad. It is so simple to prepare, and the taste is divine. Your family and friends will be begging you for this recipe!

1. Cut the avocado in half and remove the seed. Discarding the shell, scoop out the flesh and place it in a food processor.

2. Add the remaining ingredients to the food processor and pulse until completely smooth. If necessary, add cool water 1 tablespoon at a time until the desired consistency is reached.

3. Use the dressing immediately, or transfer to a container and refrigerate until ready to use.

chimichurri Dressing

Yield: About I cup

3 green onions

2 cloves garlic

1/2 cup cold pressed extra virgin olive oil

1/4 cup chopped fresh Italian parsley

1/4 cup chopped fresh cilantro

3 tablespoons freshly squeezed lemon juice

1/2 teaspoon sea salt

Chimichurri is a classic Argentinean green sauce, made with fresh herbs and olive oil. It is extremely versatile, and functions beautifully as both an accompaniment to main courses and as a salad dressing.

1. Place all of the ingredients in a food processor and blend until smooth.

2. Use the dressing immediately, or transfer to a container and refrigerate until ready to use. If refrigerating, allow the dressing to return to room temperature and stir vigorously before using.

TASTES GREAT WITH . . .

"Ceviche" (page 135) and "Beans" and "Rice" (page 138).

Green Onion Sauce

Yield: About 2 cups

I cup raw or untoasted pine nuts

3 large scallions, coarsely chopped (about I cup)

1/4 cup cold pressed extra virgin olive oil

3 tablespoons freshly squeezed lemon juice

1/2 teaspoon dry mustard seeds

My favorite Argentinean grill serves this sauce over whitefish. Not only is it creamy and delicious, its beautiful color sparks the presentation of any meal.

1. Place the pine nuts in a food processor and pulse until completely blended. Add the remaining ingredients and pulse until fully combined.

2. Use the sauce immediately, or transfer to a container and refrigerate until ready to use. If refrigerating, allow the sauce to return to room temperature and stir vigorously before serving.

"Ceviche" with Chimichurri

Ceviche is a popular South American dish in which fish is cooked with lime juice and salt. For this adaptation, I substitute sweet jicama for the fish and add Chimichurri Dressing, which is very common in Argentina. This is an outstanding dish that will surely impress raw foodie friends and skeptics alike. I recommend using a mandolin slicer to cut the jicama, but a sharp knife can be used as well.

Yield: 6 to 8 servings

2 large jicama

3 tablespoons freshly squeezed lime juice

3 tablespoons cold pressed extra virgin olive oil

$^1/_2$ teaspoon salt

1 cup Chimichurri Dressing (page 134)

1. Peel the jicama, then cut them into very thin slices no more than $^1/_8$ inch thick.

2. In a container or bowl with a cover, combine the lime juice, olive oil, and salt. Add the jicama slices and mix, ensuring that each slice is thoroughly coated. Cover, transfer to the refrigerator, and let marinate for 24 hours.

3. To serve, place 5 or 6 pieces of jicama on a plate and drizzle with Chimichurri Dressing. Enjoy!

FOR A CHANGE . . .

- Sprinkle chopped tomatoes and scallions over each serving.

Spinach and Dandelion Tart

Yield: 8-inch tart

- - - - - - - - - - -

Crust

$1/2$ cup sun-dried tomatoes

1 cup warm water

2 carrots, peeled and roughly chopped (about $1 1/2$ cups)

2 cloves garlic

2 cups fresh corn kernels, or frozen and thawed

1 cup ground flax seed

2 tablespoons freshly squeezed lemon juice

1 teaspoon sea salt

1 teaspoon ground cumin

Filling

1 cup coarsely chopped spinach leaves

1 cup coarsely chopped dandelion leaves

2 tablespoons freshly squeezed lemon juice

2 tablespoons chopped basil

1 tablespoon cold pressed extra virgin olive oil

1 teaspoon sea salt

$1/2$ teaspoon black pepper

This tart is a light dish that is perfect served alone or with a salad. I like to double this recipe and make it over the weekend, so that it is readily available as a quick and healthy snack all week long.

1. To make the crust, soak the tomatoes in the water for 1 hour, or until soft. Reserving the soaking liquid, drain the tomatoes and place them in a food processor.

2. Add the remaining crust ingredients except the soak water to the food processor and mix until smooth. If necessary, add the reserved tomato water 1 or 2 tablespoons at a time until the crust has a dough-like consistency.

3. Place the dough on the center of a Teflex dehydrator sheet. With the back of a large spoon, spread out the dough into an 8-inch circle. Using your fingers, build up the sides of the circle until it resembles a pizza crust. Place in the dehydrator and dehydrate at 105°F for 12 hours. (If you don't own a dehydrator, see page 5 for instructions on how to use an oven for this purpose.)

4. Flip the crust (see page 6 for flipping instructions) and then carefully remove the top Teflex sheet and return the crust to the dehydrator. Dehydrate an additional 4 to 6 hours, or until the desired crunchiness is reached.

5. About 30 minutes before serving, place all the filling ingredients in a medium bowl and mix to combine. Let sit for 30 minutes at room temperature.

6. Remove the crust from the dehydrator and fill with the spinach filling. Cut into wedges and serve.

FOR A CHANGE . . .

• Add any or all of the following toppings to the tart before serving: $1/_2$ cup chopped tomatoes, $1/_2$ cup crumbled raw goat cheese, 2 tablespoons fresh chopped oregano leaves, or Tomatillo Salsa (page 130).

Corn Chowder With "Bacon" Bits

This corn chowder is a hearty raw version of a classic South American treat. The "bacon" bits, made with jicama, add an extra kick to this satisfying dish. I recommend using a mandolin slicer to cut the jicama, but you can also use a sharp knife.

1. To make the "bacon," use a mandolin slicer to cut the jicama into slices that are $1/_8$ inch thin. Then, cut the slices into approximately 1-inch squares.

2. In a medium bowl, combine the miso, Bragg, cumin, and water. Add the jicama and mix, ensuring that each piece is coated.

3. Lay the jicama on dehydrator sheets and dehydrate at 105°F for 24 hours. (If you don't own a dehydrator, see page 5 for instructions on how to use an oven for this purpose.)

4. Just before serving, place all the chowder ingredients in a food processor and blend until smooth and creamy.

5. Ladle the chowder into bowls and distribute the bacon on top of each serving. Serve and enjoy!

FOR A CHANGE . . .

• Sprinkle additional chopped fresh cilantro over each serving.

Yield: 4 to 6 servings

"Bacon" Bits

$1/_2$ medium jicama

1 tablespoon white miso

1 tablespoon Bragg Liquid Aminos or tamari soy sauce

1 teaspoon ground cumin

1 teaspoon water

Chowder

2 cloves garlic, coarsely chopped

1 stalk celery, coarsely chopped

$1/_2$ medium red bell pepper, chopped

2 cups fresh corn kernels, or frozen and thawed

1 cup water

1 cup raw or untoasted pine nuts

$1/_2$ cup chopped fresh cilantro

1 teaspoon freshly squeezed lime juice

Black "Beans" and "Rice"

No South American collection of recipes would be complete without a version of this staple meal. Using sunflower seeds for the beans and parsnips for the rice transforms this classic dish into an easily digestible treat that fits into any raw food diet plan.

Yield: 6 to 8 servings

Black "Beans"

1 cup sunflower seeds

4 cups cool water

1 cup sun-dried tomatoes

1 teaspoon chipotle chili powder

$1/2$ teaspoon red chili pepper flakes

$1/4$ cup chopped fresh cilantro

"Rice"

2 medium parsnips, peeled and coarsely chopped (about 2 cups)

1 cup coarsely chopped daikon

$1/2$ cup raw or untoasted pine nuts

$1/2$ cup chopped fresh cilantro

$1/2$ cup chopped fresh Italian parsley

3 teaspoons freshly squeezed lemon juice

$1/2$ teaspoon sea salt

$1/2$ teaspoon ground cumin

1. To prepare the "beans," place the sunflower seeds in 2 cups of the water and let soak for 4 hours. Drain and rinse the seeds and set them aside.

2. Place the sun-dried tomatoes in the remaining 2 cups of water and let soak for 1 hour, or until soft. Reserving the soaking water, drain the tomatoes.

3. Place the seeds and the tomatoes in a food processor and pulse until the mixture is well-blended, but still chunky.

4. Transfer the bean mixture to a large bowl. Add the chipotle chili powder, red chili pepper flakes, cilantro, and $1/2$ cup of the reserved tomato water. Stir to combine, then set aside.

5. To make the "rice," place the parsnips, daikon, and pine nuts in a food processor and pulse just until the mixture resembles rice-like coarse crumbs. (Watch closely, as there isn't much time between the coarse rice mixture and a blended paste!)

6. Transfer the rice to a medium bowl. Add the cilantro, parsley, lemon juice, salt, and cumin, and gently mix by hand.

7. Place a scoop of rice alongside a scoop of beans and serve.

TASTES GREAT WITH . . .

Brazilian Cucumber Salad (page 132), Chilean Tomato Salad (page 133), or a fresh green salad with Creamy Cumin and Avocado Dressing (page 133) for a more complete meal.

FOR A CHANGE . . .

● Use 1 cup coarsely chopped cauliflower instead of daikon to make the rice.

Daikon "Scallops" With Green Onion Sauce

Marinated daikon takes on the role of fish in this recipe. A Green Onion Sauce topping gives this dish a delicious Argentinean flavor.

1. Peel the daikon and slice them into rounds that are $1/4$ inch thick. Set aside.

2. In a medium bowl, combine the garlic, honey, lemon juice, and salt. Add the daikon rounds, mix, and let marinate for 2 to 3 days in the refrigerator.

3. To serve, place 3 or 4 daikon "scallops" on a plate and top with Green Onion Sauce.

Yield: 4 to 6 servings

2 daikon

2 cloves garlic, diced

2 tablespoons raw honey

2 tablespoons freshly squeezed lemon juice

$1/8$ teaspoon sea salt

1 cup Green Onion Sauce (page 134)

FOR A CHANGE . . .

● Use Mustard Sauce (page 113) instead of Green Onion Sauce.

● Top with diced scallions and 1 tablespoon minced shallot.

South American Marinade

Yield: About $1/2$ cup

. . . .

3 cloves garlic, finely diced

$1/2$ jalapeño pepper, seeded and finely diced, with white membranes removed

$1/2$ onion, thinly sliced (about $1/2$ cup)

$1/2$ cup chopped fresh Italian parsley

$1/4$ cup cold pressed extra virgin olive oil

3 tablespoons freshly squeezed lime juice

$1/2$ teaspoon sea salt

$1/2$ teaspoon black pepper

Vegetable of choice

In South America, vegetables are often marinated before they are served. This versatile marinade pairs well with any vegetable, always bringing out a fantastic flavor.

1. Place all of the ingredients except the vegetable in a large bowl. Mix gently to combine.

2. Add the vegetable of your choice and let marinate at room temperature for at least 20 minutes. For a stronger flavor, leave the vegetables in the marinade for up to 1 hour before serving.

TIP . . .

Limes can be stored in the refrigerator for up to two weeks.

Churros

Churros are a typical South American pastry. They are usually made with potato flour, fried in oil, and eaten for breakfast. For this recipe, I use sprouted wheat berries instead of flour, resulting in a fun treat that is so light, it can be eaten guiltlessly for breakfast!

Yield: 10 to 12 churros

. . . .

$^3/_4$ cup dates

$1^1/_2$ cup water

$^1/_2$ cup raw or untoasted almonds

2 cups sprouted wheat berries (see page 30 for sprouting instructions)

2 teaspoons organic vanilla extract

Coating

$^1/_4$ cup finely ground raw or untoasted cashews

1 tablespoon ground cinnamon

1. Place the dates in the water and let soak for 1 hour, or until soft. Reserving the water, drain the dates and set aside.

2. Place the almonds in a food processor and pulse to a fine powder. Add the wheat berries, dates, and vanilla, and mix until smooth and creamy. If necessary, add the reserved water 1 tablespoon at a time until the mixture has a cookie dough consistency. Transfer to a sealable plastic storage bag and set aside.

3. In a medium bowl, prepare the coating by combining the cashews and cinnamon. Set aside.

4. To make a churro, cut a $^1/_4$-inch opening in the corner of the plastic bag containing the dough. Squeeze out the dough onto Teflex dehydrator sheets into log shapes about $2^1/_2$ inches long. Sprinkle the dough with the cashew and cinnamon mixture and dehydrate at 105°F for 24 hours or until the desired crunchiness is reached. (If you don't own a dehydrator, see page 5 for instructions on how to use an oven for this purpose.)

5. Remove the churros from the dehydrator and serve warm.

TIP . . .

The churros taste best served warm, right after dehydrating. However, if you don't have time to dehydrate for the full 24 hours, the churros can be removed from the dehydrator and refrigerated for up to one week in a sealed plastic container. Simply warm them up in the dehydrator for 30 minutes at 112°F before you want to eat them.

"Tres Leche" Banana Layer Treat

Typically, tres leche cake is made by soaking a sponge cake in a combination of three types of milk, which makes for a very dense, high-calorie dessert. For this recipe, I have substituted cashew and pine nut cream for the dairy cream and added some layers of raw banana cake for an absolutely amazing raw dessert that is so incredibly rich, a small piece will leave you satisfied.

Yield: 4- to 5-inch cake

2 cups raw or untoasted pine nuts

3 bananas, peeled

$1/4$ cup water

2 teaspoons organic vanilla extract

"Tres Leche" Cream

2 cups raw or untoasted cashews

1 cup raw or untoasted pine nuts

$1/2$ cup dried coconut

$1/4$ cup raw honey

4 tablespoons freshly squeezed lemon juice

1 teaspoon organic vanilla extract

1. To make the cake layers, place the pine nuts in a food processor and pulse to a fine powder. Add the bananas, water, and vanilla, and pulse until smooth.

2. Spoon 5 equal portions of batter onto Teflex dehydrator sheets, and spread each into a circle. Dehydrate at 105°F for 24 hours. (If you don't own a dehydrator, see page 5 for instructions on how to use an oven for this purpose.) Flip the cakes, then remove the Teflex sheets and return the cakes to the dehydrator for 4 more hours, or until the cakes resemble fruit leather (like a Fruit Roll-Up).

3. For the filling, place the cashews and pine nuts in a food processor and pulse until they are finely ground. Add the coconut, honey, lemon juice, and vanilla. Mix until smooth and creamy.

4. Assemble the layers by placing one of the cake layers on a plate. Top it with 2 tablespoons of filling and spread thin. Top this with another layer of banana cake and continue until all of the cake and filling ingredients are used, ending with a cake on top. Serve.

TASTES GREAT WITH . . .

Coconut Ice Cream (page 124).

TIP . . .

This treat packs a lot of punch for its size! Cut the cake in two, three, or four pieces for an incredibly satisfying mini-dessert.

Cocadas

*Cocadas are classic coconut macaroons with
a South American twist. This raw version is
very simple and absolutely delicious.*

Yield: 12 to 15 cookies

1 cup dates

2 cups water

2 cups raw or untoasted
walnuts

2 cups dried coconut

1 teaspoon organic vanilla
extract

1. Place the dates in the water and let soak for 1 hour, or until soft. Reserving the water, drain the dates and set aside.

2. Place the walnuts in a food processor and pulse until they are a fine powder. Add the coconut, dates, and vanilla, and blend until completely combined. If necessary, add the reserved water 1 tablespoon at a time until the mixture has a cookie dough consistency.

3. Drop the dough by rounded teaspoons onto Teflex dehydrator sheets. Dehydrate at 105°F for 24 hours.

4. Remove from the dehydrator and serve warm, or refrigerate and serve cold at a later time.

Banana Pineapple Sorbet

*This satisfying and delicious dessert is simple,
quick, and sweet—the perfect combination!*

Yield: About 4 cups

3 bananas, peeled and frozen

1 cup pineapple chunks

$1/4$ cup water

1 teaspoon organic vanilla
extract

1. Place all the ingredients in a food processor or high speed blender and combine until completely smooth.

2. Serve immediately, or place back in the freezer for 1 hour if you prefer an icier texture.

METRIC CONVERSION TABLES

COMMON LIQUID CONVERSIONS

Measurement	=	Milliliters
1/4 teaspoon	=	1.25 milliliters
1/2 teaspoon	=	2.50 milliliters
3/4 teaspoon	=	3.75 milliliters
1 teaspoon	=	5.00 milliliters
1 1/4 teaspoons	=	6.25 milliliters
1 1/2 teaspoons	=	7.50 milliliters
1 3/4 teaspoons	=	8.75 milliliters
2 teaspoons	=	10.0 milliliters
1 tablespoon	=	15.0 milliliters
2 tablespoons	=	30.0 milliliters

Measurement	=	Liters
1/4 cup	=	0.06 liters
1/2 cup	=	0.12 liters
3/4 cup	=	0.18 liters
1 cup	=	0.24 liters
1 1/4 cups	=	0.30 liters
1 1/2 cups	=	0.36 liters
2 cups	=	0.48 liters
2 1/2 cups	=	0.60 liters
3 cups	=	0.72 liters
3 1/2 cups	=	0.84 liters
4 cups	=	0.96 liters
4 1/2 cups	=	1.08 liters
5 cups	=	1.20 liters
5 1/2 cups	=	1.32 liters

CONVERTING FAHRENHEIT TO CELSIUS

Fahrenheit	=	Celsius
200–205	=	95
220–225	=	105
245–250	=	120
275	=	135
300–305	=	150
325–330	=	165
345–350	=	175
370–375	=	190
400–405	=	205
425–430	=	220
445–450	=	230
470–475	=	245
500	=	260

CONVERSION FORMULAS

LIQUID

When You Know	Multiply By	To Determine
teaspoons	5.0	milliliters
tablespoons	15.0	milliliters
fluid ounces	30.0	milliliters
cups	0.24	liters
pints	0.47	liters
quarts	0.95	liters

WEIGHT

When You Know	Multiply By	To Determine
ounces	28.0	grams
pounds	0.45	kilograms

RESOURCES

The following well-established companies, websites, schools, and organizations are outstanding resources for anyone interested in a raw food diet. They offer information, equipment, supplies, and/or ingredients to make the most of this dietary lifestyle.

ORGANIZATIONS AND LEARNING CENTERS

Hippocrates Health Institute
1443 Palmdale Court
West Palm Beach, FL 33441
(561) 471-8876
www.hippocratesinst.org

Founded by Ann Wigmore in the 1950s, this retreat center is a leader in the field of wellness programs and natural healthcare.

Lisa's Living Well
(603) 340-3983
www.lisaslivingwell.com

This is my personal website, which I established due to the overwhelming interest and response I had witnessed to the raw food dietary lifestyle. This site offers information on a wide variety of raw food courses including un-cooking classes, retreats, and consultations.

Living Light Culinary Arts Institute
301-B North Main Street
Fort Bragg, CA 95437
(707) 964-2420
(800) 816-2319
www.rawfoodchef.com

This California-based un-cooking school features training and workshops for the aspiring raw food chef.

Tree of Life Rejuvenation Center
PO Box 778
Patagonia, AZ 85624
(866) 394-2520
www.treeoflife.nu

Founded in 1993, this is the "world's leading spiritual, vegan, raw and live food retreat center." A variety of spiritual and nutritional education programs are among its many offerings.

FOOD AND KITCHEN EQUIPMENT

Amazon
www.amazon.com

Along with books on nutrition and raw foods (including those on the Recommended Reading list that follows), Amazon's website is an outstanding source of kitchen equipment and utensils. It offers a wide variety of brands and styles at competitive prices. All of the equipment listed in Chapter 1—both essential and optional—can be found on this site.

Breville
(866) 273-8455
www.breville.com

This international company sells a line of reliable, high-quality juicers, including a mid-priced, professional-style model that has an extra-wide feed tube for juicing whole fruits and vegetables.

Crate and Barrel
(800) 967-6696
www.crateandbarrel.com

This company offers a wide variety of good-quality kitchen essentials. Its line of food containers is perfect for storing all of your raw foods and raw food dishes.

Champion Juicers
(Plastaket Mfg. Co., Inc.)
6220 E. Highway 12
Lodi, CA 95240
(209) 369-2154
(866) 935-8423
www.championjuicer.com

Considered by many to be the ultimate juicing machine, the Champion Juicer has a powerful motor and is capable of extracting large quantities of juice from fruits and vegetables.

Eden Foods, Inc.
701 Tecumseh Road
Clinton, MI 49236
(888) 424-3336
www.edenfoods.com

This natural food company, which has been family owned and operated since 1968, is dedicated to providing the finest whole food from only trusted growers and processors. It offers a variety of products and ingredients, including hard to find sea vegetables.

FoodieLoot
http://foodieloot.ecrater.com/

This company carries over ninety premium-quality organic herbs, spices, and blends for any type of cuisine. It also carries a variety of teas, salts, oils, and specialty foods.

Green Star Juicers
www.greenstarjuicers.org

This company makes some of the best-quality juicers available. When compared to other juicers, Green Star Juicers extract the most nutrients from your fruits and vegetables.

ImportFood
PO Box 2054
Issaquah, WA 98027
(888) 618-8424
www.importfood.com

ImportFood is a great source for ordering spices, condiments, and herbs, including those that can be hard to find.

Jack LaLanne's Power Juicer
(973) 287-5150
www.powerjuicer.com

This mid-level juicer is both relatively efficient and moderately priced. It is a great choice for those who are new to a raw food diet.

live live & organic
261 East 10th Street
New York City, NY 10009
(212) 505-5504
(877) 505-5504
www.live-live.com

Along with providing helpful information about raw food diets, this company also offers a wide variety of products, including juicers, dehydrators, and hard-to-find ingredients. It even has a raw skin-care line!

Navitas Naturals
9 Pamaron Way, Suite J
Novato, CA 94949
(888) 645-4282
www.navitasnaturals.com

This company provides premium organic functional foods that increase energy and enhance health. It has a variety of products that are rich in antioxidants, vitamins, and minerals.

The Raw Food World
(866) 729-3438
www.therawfoodworld.com

This is a good place to purchase raw food ingredients, including a number of hard-to-find sea vegetables. It

also offers a huge selection of books, as well as kitchen equipment, such as juicers, food processors, and spiralizers.

RawGuru
(800) 577-4729
www.rawguru.com

This company offers everything you need to start or continue a raw food diet, including kitchen equipment and a wide selection of ingredients and snack foods.

Spice It Up
www.spiceituponline.com

This website features over 250 spices, rubs, and chilies, as well as exotic "superfoods" like raw cacao powder and goji berries.

Williams-Sonoma, Inc.
(877) 812-6235
www.williams-sonoma.com

A specialty retailer of gourmet cookware, Williams-Sonoma offers high-quality kitchen equipment. It carries most of the equipment—both essential and optional—listed in Chapter 1.

SPROUTING AND GARDEN SUPPLIES

AeroGrow International, Inc.
6075 Longbow Drive, Suite 200
Boulder, CO 80301
(303) 444-7755
www.aerogrow.com

This company sells a variety of indoor AeroGardens, which allow plants to grow in an air or mist environment without soil. With these planters, you can produce garden-fresh vegetables and nutritious herbs in your kitchen year-round.

Indoor Gardening Supplies
PO Box 527
Dexter, MI 48130
(800) 823-5740
www.indoorgardensupplies.com

This company offers a wide variety of indoor gardening supplies, including seeds, plant lights, and plant stands.

Organic Gardening
(800) 666-2206
www.organicgardening.com

This company's website is a fantastic source for anyone who wants to learn more about gardening.

Sproutman
PO Box 1100
Great Barrington, MA 01230
(413) 528-5200
http://sproutman.com

The Sproutman is a great resource for information about sprouting, juicing, and fasting. It also offers sprouting appliances, seeds, and equipment.

SproutPeople
170 Mendell Street
San Francisco, CA 94124
(877) 777-6887
www.sproutpeople.com

This company offers a wide selection of organic seeds, sprouting kits, and sampler packages.

RECOMMENDED READING

The following books are just a few of my favorites on raw foods, vegetarianism, and the health of our planet. These books influenced me on my raw food journey, and I hope they have a similar effect on you.

Campbell, T. Colin and Thomas M. Campbell II. *The China Study.* Dallas, TX: BenBella Books, Inc., 2006.

Cousens, Gabriel. *Conscious Eating.* Berkeley, CA: North Atlantic Books, 2000.

Cousens, Gabriel and the Tree of Life Café Chefs. *Rainbow Green Live-Food Cuisine.* Berkeley, CA: North Atlantic Books, 2003.

Howell, Edward. *Enzyme Nutrition.* Garden City Park, NY: Avery, 1995.

Lyman, Howard F. *Mad Cowboy.* New York, NY: Touchstone, 1998.

Pollan, Michael. *In Defense of Food.* New York, NY: Penguin Group, 2008.

Robbins, John. *Diet for a New America.* Tiburon, CA: H J Kramer, Inc., 1987.

Rose, Natalia. *The Raw Food Detox Diet.* New York, NY: HarperCollins Publishers, Inc., 2005.

Vasey, Christopher. *The Acid-Alkaline Diet for Optimum Health.* Rochester, VT: Healing Arts Press, 1999.

Wigmore, Ann. *Be Your Own Doctor.* Garden City Park, NY: Avery, 1982.

Wigmore, Ann. *The Hippocrates Diet and Health Program.* Garden City Park, NY: Avery, 1983.

Wolfe, David. *Eating for Beauty.* Berkeley, CA: North Atlantic Books, 2003.

Wolfe, David. *The Sunfood Diet Success System.* San Diego, CA: Sunfood Publishing, 2008.

About the Author

Lisa Mann trained at the Natural Healing Institute of Naturopathy to become a clinical nutritionist. She is also a raw food teacher and classically trained French chef. She spent twenty years traveling the globe in her quest for fun adventures, fantastic food, and great health. Lisa is the founder of Lisa's Living Well, a company that aims to bring fantastic, easy-to-prepare healthy and raw food to the mainstream by offering raw food classes, retreats, and nutritional consultations. When she isn't working, Lisa enjoys spending time with her family, practicing yoga, bicycling, and taking long hikes in the woods.

INDEX

EAT SMART, EAT RAW

Creative Vegetarian Recipes for a Healthier Life

Kate Wood

As the popularity of raw vegetarian cuisine continues to soar, so does the mounting scientific evidence that uncooked food is amazingly good for you. From healing diseases to detoxifying your body, from lowering cholesterol to eliminating excess weight, the many important health benefits derived from such a diet are too important to ignore. Now there is another compelling reason to go raw—taste! In *Eat Smart, Eat Raw,* cook and health writer Kate Wood not only explains how to get started, but also provides delicious kitchen-tested recipes guaranteed to surprise and delight even the fussiest of eaters.

Eat Smart, Eat Raw begins by explaining the basics of cooking without heat, from choosing the best equipment to stocking your pantry. What follows are twelve recipe chapters filled with truly exceptional dishes, including hearty breakfasts, savory soups, satisfying entrées, and luscious desserts. There is even a recipe chapter on the "almost raw" for those who are a bit harder to please. Included is a list of groups, stores, and related websites that provide all the information you need to begin enjoying raw vegetarian cuisine.

Whether you are an ardent vegetarian, a health-conscious consumer, or just someone in search of a wonderful meal, *Eat Smart, Eat Raw* offers over 150 delightful recipes that may forever change the way you look at an oven.

About the Author

Kate Wood lives in Brighton, England, with her husband and three sons. She has been a committed raw foodist since 1993, and has unrivaled experience in feeding a family on the raw foods diet. She is the former editor of *Get Fresh*, the world's premier raw foods magazine, and is currently assistant editor of *Juno*, the UK natural parenting magazine. She also runs Raw Living, one of Europe's leading suppliers of raw foods, superfoods, and kitchen equipment.

$15.95 • 184 Pages • 7.5 x 9-inch quality paperback • ISBN 978-0-7570-0261-8

GREENS AND GRAINS ON THE DEEP BLUE SEA COOKBOOK

Fabulous Vegetarian Cuisine from the Holistic Holiday at Sea Cruises

Sandy Pukel and Mark Hanna

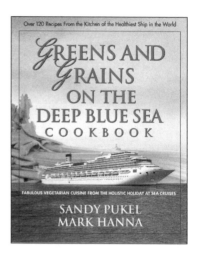

You are invited to come aboard one of America's premier health cruises. Too busy to get away? Even if you can't swim in the ship's pool, you can still enjoy its gourmet cuisine, because natural foods expert Sandy Pukel and master chef Mark Hanna have created *Greens and Grains on the Deep Blue Sea Cookbook*—a titanic collection of the most popular vegetarian dishes served aboard the Holistic Holiday at Sea cruises.

Each of the book's more than 120 recipes is designed to provide not only great taste, but also maximum nutrition. Choose from among an innovative selection of taste-tempting appetizers, soups, salads, entrées, side dishes, and desserts. Easy-to-follow instructions ensure that even novices have superb results. With *Greens and Grains on the Deep Blue Sea Cookbook* you can enjoy fabulous signature dishes from the Holistic Holiday at Sea cruises in the comfort of your own home.

$16.95 • 160 Pages • 7.5 x 9-inch quality paperback • ISBN 978-0-7570-0287-8

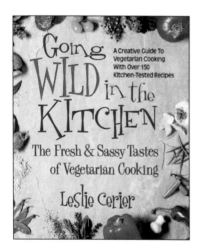

GOING WILD IN THE KITCHEN

The Fresh & Sassy Tastes of Vegetarian Cooking

Leslie Cerier

Go wild in the kitchen! Venture beyond the usual beans, grains, and vegetables to include an exciting variety of organic vegetarian fare in your meals. *Going Wild in the Kitchen,* written by expert chef Leslie Cerier, shows you how. In addition to providing helpful cooking tips and techniques, this book offers over 150 kitchen-tested recipes for taste-tempting dishes that contain such unique ingredients as edible flowers; tasty sea vegetables; wild mushrooms, berries, and herbs; and exotic ancient grains like teff, quinoa, and Chinese "forbidden" black rice. The author encourages the creative instincts of novice and seasoned cooks alike, prompting them to "go wild" in the kitchen by adding, changing, or substituting ingredients in existing recipes. To help, an extensive ingredient glossary is included, along with a wealth of helpful cooking guidelines. Lively illustrations and a complete resource list for finding organic foods completes this user-friendly cookbook.

Going Wild in the Kitchen is more than a unique cookbook—it's a recipe for inspiration. Excite your palate with this treasure-trove of distinctive, healthy, and taste-tempting recipe creations.

$16.95 • 240 Pages • 7.5 x 9-inch quality paperback • ISBN 978-0-7570-0091-1

THE COMPLETE MUFFIN COOKBOOK

The Ultimate Guide to Making Great Muffins

Gloria Ambrosia

Ah, muffins—about as perfect as food gets. These freshly baked gems are delicious, immensely satisfying, portable, and suitable for any time of day.

In *The Complete Muffin Cookbook,* expert baker Gloria Ambrosia shares an extraordinary collection of over 130 recipes for delectable muffins that are not only sensational, but also quick and easy to prepare (you can whip up a batch in less than thirty minutes). After revealing muffin-making basics, as well as the helpful tips and techniques she has gathered over the years, Gloria presents six chapters that are packed with her incredible muffin recipes. Start the day with a still-warm-from-the-oven Better Banana Nut Bran, Peachy Peach, or Chai Muffin. Or choose from a variety of sensational savory selections, such as French Onion, Mexicali Corn, and Tomato-Basil Muffins; they make delicious snacks, superb accompaniments to soups and salads, and even welcome guests at the dinner table. There is even a chapter on low-fat (but still yummy) muffins that are out of this world!

$14.95 • 216 Pages • 7.5 x 7.5-inch quality paperback • ISBN 978-0-7570-0179-6

GREAT NATURAL BREADS MADE EASY

Simple Ways to Make Healthful Bread

Bernice Hunt

Who can resist the heady aroma and fabulous flavor of freshly baked bread? Called the "staff of life" for good reason, wholesome bread has been a staple since Biblical times. Today, even though commercial breads contain more healthful natural ingredients than they did a generation ago, they just can't compete with the taste and goodness of a whole-grain loaf baked in your own oven. The problem has long been that bread making is too difficult—or so it seemed until now. Bernice Hunt's *Great Natural Breads Made Easy* is a simple-to-follow guide that enables anyone to make a spectacular loaf of artisan bread—even if they've never baked before.

From the classic whole-grain loaf, to the versatile focaccia, to the humble bagel, this book tells you exactly how to mix, knead, shape, and decorate a variety of nutritious, mouth-watering breads. To further insure success, Lauren Jarrett's illustrations show exactly how each step is performed.

$16.95 • 160 Pages • 7.5 x 9-inch quality paperback • ISBN 978-0-7570-0294-6

ENEMY OF THE STEAK

Vegetarian Recipes to Win Friends and Influence Meat-Eaters

Nikki & David Goldbeck

Don't blame vegetarians for starting this. Who said "real food for real people"? Aren't asparagus, carrots, and tomatoes every bit as real as . . . that other food? To answer the call to battle, best-selling authors Nikki and David Goldbeck have created a wonderfully tempting new cookbook that offers a wealth of kitchen-tested recipes—recipes that nourish the body, please the palate, and satisfy even the heartiest of appetites.

Enemy of the Steak first presents basic information on vegetarian cooking and stocking the vegetarian pantry. Then eight great chapters offer recipes for breakfast fare; appetizers and hors d'oeuvres; soups; salads; entrées; side dishes; sauces, toppings, and marinades; and desserts. Throughout the book, the Goldbecks have included practical tips and advice on weight loss, disease prevention, and other important topics. They also offer dozens of fascinating facts about why fruits and veggies are so good for you.

A perfect marriage of nutrition and the art of cooking, *Enemy of the Steak* is for everyone who loves a good healthy meal. Simply put, it's great food for smart people. If you have to take sides, you couldn't be in better company.

About the Authors

Nikki and *David Goldbeck* have been writing about consumer issues, health, and nutrition since 1972. They are the best-selling authors of six books, including *American Wholefoods Cuisine* and *Healthy Highways*. Nikki Goldbeck is a practicing nutritionist and food educator who holds workshops for people with heart disease, diabetes, cancer, and obesity. The Goldbecks currently live in upstate New York.

$16.95 • 248 Pages • 7.5 x 9-inch quality paperback • ISBN 978-0-7570-0273-1